T0170422

CHAMPAGNE
WITHOUT BUBBLES

Refreshing Your Soul in 31 Days

BRYAN A. ANDERSON

STORYLINE
PRESS

Storyline Press

ISBN: 9780578341910

Champagne without Bubbles
Refreshing Your Soul in 31 Days
Copyright © 2022 by Bryan A. Anderson

Cover Design by: Diana Lawrence

Manufactured in the United States of America
10 9 8 7 6 5 4 3 2 1

To Beatrice:

Your life, though short, shaped our hearts in ways
we could never imagine when you first came into this world.
You brought joy to all you met! Jesus has you now
and so our hearts are comforted.
Mom, India, and I will miss you.
We will see you in heaven soon, my Sunshine!

Love,

Dad

CONTENTS

ACKNOWLEDGMENTS

Mom and Dad, thank you! I'm grateful for the love and joyful atmosphere that you have created at home throughout my life. I'm also grateful for your comfort during life's most bitter moments.

Paul, thank you! Your insightful comments shaped major sections of this devotional and has deeply impacted me, the writer, as I fleshed out the additions.

Patrick, thank you! Our decades-long friendship and ministry together have meant the world to me!

Duane, thank you! You have been my closest and dearest friend since youth! You have been there during life's grandest moments as well as it's darkest days. I am honored to know you my brother!

Stephen, Dan, and Silas, thank you! Our many years of prayer and fasting for a great spiritual awakening of the people of Wall Street was the foundation for this book. Apart from that spiritual work, there would be no book! Thank you!

Garth, thank you! You made church history come to life. The teachings on revival and Richard Baxter's life and works shaped important sections of this book.

USING THIS BOOK

Champagne without Bubbles is a 31-day devotional for those thirsty for God to bring spiritual vitality to their lives especially when life seems broken. While the book was written with a Christian audience in mind, the book is accessible to all who have experienced the pain, disappointments, and struggles of life and wonder if there is something that will fill life with hope, purpose, and love.

Each of the 31 daily readings is structured the same. A Champagne analogy introduces each spiritual topic. The spiritual topic is then explored from the viewpoint of the struggles we face and the wisdom and guidance we receive from God's Word. A closing prayer then follows. To assist with making the daily reading a reality in our lives, I conclude with three suggestions: Scripture to meditate upon, a worship song I hope will resonate with the heart, and several simple ideas ("tips") to take action.

The Champagne theme was selected for one primary reason: Champagne is the drink of choice to celebrate life's greatest and grandest of moments as well as ushering in a new year full of hope and new beginnings. This is analogous with the spiritual vitality, hope, and effervescence that God brings about in renewing our lives.

Ezekiel 37:1–14 (The Valley of Dry Bones) is one of the Bible's classic texts on spiritual renewal and was chosen as the backbone for each day's reading. The "dry bones" are synonymous with the things that are broken in our lives. Each day's reading incorporates Ezekiel's valley of dry bones and is used as a transition point between the broken areas in life and the path God calls us to follow that leads to spiritual refreshment.

The contrast between Champagne and dry bones is intentional to help the reader contrast the "spiritual waste-land" of the current situation with the refreshing "streams of living water" offered by God. God shows us our dry bones because He wants to do something with them—to renew them, to give them life, to put the bubbles in our lives.

My prayer is that as you read through each day and apply its lessons to your life you will experience the following: personal intimacy with the triune God;[1] spiritual wholeness, healing, and renewal; and a life overflowing with life-giving bubbles.

INTRODUCTION

W hen you open a bottle of Champagne, the first thing you think of is celebration. Images of weddings, New Year's Eve gatherings, sports championships, anniversaries, birthday milestones, and major business deals may immediately come to mind. It is during these rare moments in life where a refreshing bottle of Champagne truly captures the joy and hopefulness of the festive occasion.

The most obvious feature that makes Champagne distinct (or any sparkling wine for that matter) is the bubbles. The bubbles are what give this wine its vivaciousness, its splendor, its spirited joyfulness and luster. What you may not know is that the bubbles are the result of a second fermentation the Champagne goes through (the first fermentation turns the grape juice into wine, the second creates the bubbles). The second fermentation does not happen naturally, it requires a Champagne maker to initiate the process. It is the hands of the Champagne maker that make the bubbles possible. Without the Champagne maker initiating the second fermentation, you are left with a naturally acidic, austere, lifeless, bone-dry, flat wine. Champagne minus the bubbles is nothing to celebrate.

Maybe the image of Champagne before the second fermentation describes an area in your life right now. Maybe it describes your whole life. There is something that is lifeless, hopeless, acidic in your life. Maybe it is your relationship with your spouse, your child, or your parent. Maybe it is your finances or work or a dream you had that is now bone dry. Maybe life is currently austere for you. Maybe it has been harsh for many years, perhaps decades. For you there is nothing to celebrate in this area of your life—only mourning, a sense of despair, fruitlessness, or defeat.

Maybe what God showed the prophet Ezekiel in the sixth century BC is an image that describes where you are right now in life,

> The hand of the LORD was on me, and he brought me out by the Spirit of the LORD and set me in the middle of a valley; it was full of bones. He led me back and forth among them, and I saw a great many bones on the floor of the valley, bones that were very dry. (Ezekiel 37:1–2)

The image was a symbol of what the Israelites were experiencing in captivity in Babylon (located in modern-day Iraq), a place far from their home in Jerusalem. The Lord told Ezekiel: "Son of man, these bones are the people of Israel. They say, 'Our bones are dried up and our hope is gone; we are cut off'" (Ezekiel 37:11). That might be you right now. Your "bones" are "dried up," your "hope is gone," and you feel "cut off" from the life you once had or where you want to be in life right now. In fact, it describes most people at some point in their lives, maybe multiple times. It is during these moments in life that we all need to go through a second fermentation, a spiritual renewal in our lives. We need to ask God to initiate the process, to make something that is lifeless in our lives into something that "bubbles."

It is the very nature of God to bring renewal to the dead things in our lives. God was not showing Ezekiel these dry bones to be spiteful. On the contrary, God showed Ezekiel these dry bones because He was planning to bring spiritual renewal to His people Israel. Nor does God show us our dry bones with the intention to leave us to wallow in our misery. Instead, God reveals our dry bones because He is planning to do something brand-new with them! In the same way the Champagne maker causes the second fermentation, we can experience the "bubbles" of a renewed life when we allow God to get involved in our "valley" full of "dry bones."

EZEKIEL 37:1–14

The hand of the LORD was on me, and he brought me out by the Spirit of the Lord and set me in the middle of a valley; it was full of bones. He led me back and forth among them, and I saw a great many bones on the floor of the valley, bones that were very dry. He asked me, "Son of man, can these bones live?"

I said, "Sovereign LORD, you alone know."

Then he said to me, "Prophesy to these bones and say to them, 'Dry bones, hear the word of the LORD! This is what the Sovereign LORD says to these bones: I will make breath enter you, and you will come to life. I will attach tendons to you and make flesh come upon you and cover you with skin; I will put breath in you, and you will come to life. Then you will know that I am the LORD.'"

So I prophesied as I was commanded. And as I was prophesying, there was a noise, a rattling sound, and the bones came together, bone to bone. I looked, and tendons and flesh appeared on them and skin covered them, but there was no breath in them.

Then he said to me, "Prophesy to the breath; prophesy, son of man, and say to it, 'This is what the Sovereign Lord says: Come, breath, from the four winds and breathe into these slain, that they may live.'" So I prophesied as he commanded me, and breath entered them; they came to life and stood up on their feet—a vast army.

Then he said to me: "Son of man, these bones are the people of Israel. They say, 'Our bones are dried up and our hope is gone; we are cut off.' Therefore prophesy and say to them: 'This is what the Sovereign Lord says: My people, I am going to open your graves and bring you up from them; I will bring you back to the land of Israel. Then you, my people, will know that I am the Lord, when I open your graves and bring you up from them. I will put my Spirit in you and you will live, and I will settle you in your own land. Then you will know that I the Lord have spoken, and I have done it, declares the Lord.'"

"See, I am doing a new thing!
Now it springs up; do you not perceive it?"

Isaiah 43:19

YOUR FIRST TASTE OF CHAMPAGNE

A New Start Requires
Forgetting the Past

T he Sound of Music is one of the most cherished movies of
all time.[2] Many of us have seen it multiple times as kids
and then enjoyed it once again with our own children.
One of the warmest and light-hearted songs, "So Long,
Farewell," was set during the great ball that Captain von
Trapp threw on the eve of his engagement to the Baroness.
The song was performed exclusively by his children with
Maria on the guitar. The playful refrain is, "So long, farewell, *au revoir, auf weidersehen*." Then between the main
refrain, each child steps out one by one to say something
cute to their father and head to bed. When it is Liesl's turn
(the eldest daughter), she sings: "I'd like to stay and taste my
first champagne." And going up to her father, Liesl says,

1

"Yes?" And of course, in a playful yet stern voice, he responds, "No," to the joy and laughter of all in attendance at the grand gala.

What a tender and loving moment shared between the father and all his children. In a room full of people, of friends and strangers alike, the focal point was on the father and his children as if they were the only ones in the room. But it was not always that way. Until Maria showed up, the family was broken. After the untimely death of his wife, the children's mother, many years earlier, Captain von Trapp had inadvertently become emotionally and physically unavailable to his children in the ensuing years. He ran the home with the military precision of a navy ship and delegated the raising of his children to a revolving door of governesses, until Maria arrived in her old dress with her luggage in one hand and her guitar in the other. It was Maria who brought life, song, and love back into the family which began deep healing between father and children as well as a future wife and mother, respectively. In the same way, it is God who brings life, song, and love into our lives when we allow Him to heal our brokenness.

The hardest step for any of us to take to move on from our brokenness is leaving our past behind. The past has a way of gripping our minds and hearts as we ruminate on our memories. There will be poor decisions we wish we could undo and wonderful moments we will never be able to reclaim. There will also be tragic situations that were out of our control and ability to stop, as well as opportunities that somehow eluded us even though they seemed to be in our very grasp. These are the dry bones of our past we have alphabetized and stored away neatly in Ezekiel's valley.

Anticipating a time that His people would experience enormous heartache and brokenness and would be grieving their past, God gave these words of instruction, encouragement, and comfort to the nation of Israel, through the prophet Isaiah:

> "Forget the former things;
>   do not dwell on the past.
> See, I am doing a new thing!
> Now it springs up; do you not perceive it?
> I am making a way in the wilderness
>   and streams in the wasteland." (Isaiah 43:18–19)

If we spend our days lingering on these former memories and trying to recapture what has been lost, we will miss the "new thing" God is planning to do in our lives.

We are not to dwell among the winter shadows of decaying tree stumps when God has planted the seeds of a grand forest, saplings even now awakening and emerging in the early spring warmth. Trying to bring the past back to life is a fruitless endeavor. Nurturing the new growth God has brought out of the barren land will, on the other hand, yield an abundant harvest.

Take time to grieve the past and release it into your Lord's hands. Take your focus away from yesteryears and even last night and the places where you once dwelt. Instead look intently at the Lord to comfort and renew your heart and ask for new eyes to see the magnificent "way in the wilderness" and the abundant "streams in the wasteland" that He has prepared specifically for you!

Lord, my past cannot be changed or reclaimed, but You are the God who makes all things new. Search me and bring to my mind every fleeting shadow of my past I am holding on to that I need to release to You. Lord, I now surrender each and every thing You bring to my mind. I trust You have my best in mind and I need not cling to these past things any longer. Thank You for making me spiritually free and healthy again. Now Lord, give me eyes to see the new things You have prepared for me and give me the courage to embrace the new adventures You have in store for me today and all the days You give and set before me. Amen!

Meditation: "Forget the former things; do not dwell on the past. See, I am doing a new thing! Now it springs up; do you not perceive it? I am making a way in the wilderness and streams in the wasteland." (Isaiah 43:18–19)

Worship: "Healing Begins" (Tenth Avenue North)

Tips: It takes time to heal the past and move into a new chapter of life! Resist the temptation to grab ahold of the new thing you believe God is doing in your life by putting all your energies into that new thing immediately. Saplings require time to grow into trees! So slow down. God knows we can easily mask our pain by grabbing the new thing He is doing in our lives instead of leaning into Him for comfort. I have found it helpful to take long walks through God's creation and talk with God about my heartaches. I have also found some of my most meaningful times with God are during long runs.

"... Indeed, the water I give them will become in them a spring
of water welling up to eternal life."

John 4:14

DAY 2

REFRESHING THE CHAMPAGNE GLASS

A Rejuvenated Heart
Requires Jesus

Watching the bubbles come up from the bottom of a glass full of Champagne is mesmerizing. Did you know that the bubbles are not uniform across Champagne makers or sparkling wine producers? Bubbles can vary in size, frequency, velocity, and duration. Even for the same bottle, temperature can also influence the bubbles. However, if you wait long enough, eventually the bubbles will die out and the sparkle will fade until the last of the CO_2 is spent from the glass. The only way to rekindle the sparkle is to refill your glass with another pour of Champagne.

Champagne is not the only thing that can lose its sparkle. Sadly, Christians can as well when they allow their joy for the Lord to fade. Our joy fades when we allow ourselves to be distracted or captivated by other pursuits or by sin. Our peace fades when difficulties, pressures, and anxieties in life dominate our thoughts. Revelation 2:1–7 cautions us that even those who appear to have a robust faith can easily forsake their first love if they are not careful to cultivate their love for Him each day. The windswept plains of Ezekiel's valley are filled with the once-vibrant, faithful followers of Christ, now left wandering aimlessly and purposelessly among the dry bones. You see, Jesus has not left us! We have left Him! Perhaps that is where you are at this moment in life. Your once-vibrant love for Jesus has fallen flat and life has lost its luster. Life seems hard. Things might be dark for you right now with no visible light in the near future. The compelling vision of Christ that once captivated your life has grown dry and the Lord seems distant to you now. You may be wondering whether your love for Jesus can be rekindled, whether that fire you once had for Him can again blaze with passion. If the reality of Christ in your life is not growing more each day, it is time to make a change.

Each day, our Lord calls us to refresh ourselves in His love and surrender our will to His all-sufficient grace and plan for that day. That is the key to getting out of the valley of dry bones—committing our hearts to do His will for that day regardless of the cost. Jesus said,

> "As the Father has loved me, so have I loved you. Now remain in my love. If you keep my commands, you will remain in my love, just as I have kept my Father's commands and remain in his love. I have told you this so that my joy may be in you and that your joy may be complete. My command is this: Love each other as I have loved you." (John 15:9–12)

Finding the place where Jesus is the center of all our focus is our most essential task each day. He must be the reason we wake up each day, to know Him better today than yesterday, and carry out His work in this world and be His witness. We must seek to be filled each day with the Holy Spirit. For without the power of the Spirit coming through our lives, we cannot serve the Lord. We must wait eagerly by His door each morning for His direction. He needs to be the inspiration for how we treat our spouses, our children, our neighbors, our employers, and our employees. Is Jesus honored by you and your actions toward others? Is He the central thought and compelling idea in your life? Jesus said, "This is to my Father's glory, that you bear much fruit, showing yourselves to be my disciples" (John 15:8).

Make each day a Jesus day, a day you refresh your love for Him and for His work in this world, and your life will be like "a spring of water, welling up to eternal life" (John 4:14). Just like those mesmerizing Champagne bubbles, your life should be bubbling up in such a way that people can be mesmerized by the effervescence and freshness of Jesus displayed through your life. After all, your identity is that of a Christian.

Jesus, forgive me for allowing my love for You to grow cold. Fill me with Your Holy Spirit. Breathe fresh life into me. Give me a passion to know and love You better and use me to bring Your effervescent love to those You send my way today. Amen.

Meditation: "As the Father has loved me, so have I loved you. Now remain in my love. If you keep my commands, you will remain in my love, just as I have kept my Father's commands and remain in his love. I have told you this so that my joy may be in you and that your joy may be complete. My command is this: Love each other as I have loved you." (John 15:9–12)

Worship: "Only Jesus" (Casting Crowns)

Tips: Don't set any expectations during your time with Jesus. Just listen for Him and to His voice. He fully knows what is happening in your life and He will bring up those things most important for you to know this very moment.

vignerons (people who cultivate grapes) began grafting their European grape varieties onto an American rootstock and replanting their vineyards. Champagne itself was replanted during the early decades of the twentieth century. Today, almost all Champagne grape vines have an American rootstock. So, when you pick up that bottle of bubbly, be thankful these mighty rootstocks can defend themselves against these invasive pests.

The rootstock, of course, is responsible for sourcing and supplying all the nutrients and water the vine and grapes need to flourish. If the roots are destroyed, so are the grapes and the entire Champagne business. Not having the right rootstock is the difference between life and death—literally. It is also the same with something even more precious than grape vines—the rootstock of wisdom, God's wisdom to be precise. We have a daily choice whether to rely on the rootstock of our own counsel and the culture's fluctuating standards, or we can graft ourselves each day to the rootstock of God's unchanging, timeless, and life-giving wisdom. The verses in Proverbs 8:32–36 are the call of Wisdom and outline the choice we are presented with each day:

> "Now then, my children, listen to me;
>   blessed are those who keep my ways.
> Listen to my instruction and be wise;
>   do not disregard it.
> Blessed are those who listen to me,
>   watching daily at my doors,
>   waiting at my doorway.
> For those who find me find life
>   and receive favor from the LORD.
> But those who fail to find me harm themselves;
>   all who hate me love death."

Do we want to set our hearts on gaining God's wisdom and insight, or are we more interested in our opinions and the opinions of others? The heart set on listening to its own voice and seeking the world's counsel will find itself nestled among a lot of other dry bones with the same perspective. Ezekiel's valley specializes in those who do not consider God's wisdom to be wise but rely on their own ideas and thoughts and counsel. Now, if you enjoy the view, by all means stay, but if you are tired of things not working out in life, perhaps it's time to look intently at what God has to say concerning wisdom and how to obtain it.

His wisdom guides us along good, pleasant, and peaceful paths (Proverbs 2:9; 3:17). It warns and keeps us from the snares that trap wicked people (Proverbs 2:9–22). It is "pure; then peace-loving, considerate, submissive, full of mercy and good fruit, impartial and sincere" (James 3:17). We are considered blessed when we find it (Proverbs 3:13).

We are to take God's wisdom seriously and thoughtfully. It requires hard work and the time needed to invest by meditating on God's words, statutes, and commands. His advice is always for our benefit and for His glory. The willingness to say no and resist both our own counsel and the pressure of the culture is critical to walking in the ways of God and living life as He designed.

When we commit our ears and our hearts to understand God's wisdom, we will discover it. When we call out to Him for insight and take the time to search for it as if we were looking for some rare treasure (Proverbs 2:3–5), we will gain our prize. So start each morning grafting onto the rootstock of God's wisdom and He will lead you along beautiful paths and a life with no regrets.

Father, I need Your wisdom today. Give me a discerning heart to choose the good and reject the wrong. Show me the people I need to interact with today and keep all others away. Help me avoid temptations and the traps that would damage my walk with You. Help me keep a tight lid on my mouth today and only speak that which is beneficial and uplifting for others to hear. And whenever my mind starts behaving negatively toward someone, please bring to my mind the words of the psalmist, "Let the words of my mouth and the meditation of my heart be acceptable in your sight, O Lord, my rock and my redeemer" (Psalm 19:14 ESV). Grant me success in everything I put my hands to this day. Thank You. Amen

Meditation: For the LORD gives wisdom; from his mouth come knowledge and understanding. He holds success in store for the upright, he is a shield to those whose walk is blameless, for he guards the course of the just and protects the way of his faithful ones. Then you will understand what is right and just and fair—every good path. For wisdom will enter your heart, and knowledge will be pleasant to your soul. Discretion will protect you, and understanding will guard you. (Proverbs 2:6–11)

Worship: "King of the World" (Natalie Grant)

Tips: The book of Proverbs is a great source of wisdom. There are 31 chapters and makes for a great daily devotional during the month (whatever day it is in the month, just read the corresponding chapter). Over time you will see the benefits of this practice to your daily life.

But the fruit of the Spirit is love, joy, peace, forebearance, kindness, goodness, faithfulness, gentleness, and self-control.

Galatians 5:22–23

GREAT FRUIT PRODUCES GREAT CHAMPAGNE

A Transformative Way of Life Requires the Holy Spirit

Louis Roederer Cristal, Krug, Veuve Clicquot, and Moët & Chandon. These are some of the premium names of Champagne. These names command respect and top dollar, for they confer quality and are saved for the most special of occasions. The reason these Champagne houses are so respected is not because they have some amazing master champagne maker who is able to work magic in the cellar. Nope. The reason why these Champagnes are at the top of their class is a result of using great grapes. The quality of the fruit from the vineyard determines the ceiling for the quality of Champagne that the winemaker can create. That is why so much attention and care is given to the

on your life and do what pleases the Spirit. If you do that, your dry bones will no longer remain dry but they will be like a fruit tree producing love, joy, peace, patience, kindness, goodness, faithfulness, gentleness, and self-control (Galatians 5:22–23).

Father, I confess that my sin of timidity has ruled my life long enough and I desire to live a life full of the Holy Spirit. I desire to walk in His ways and obey the commands of my Lord and Savior. Heal me of my dry bones and breathe life in me once again so that Your kingdom will expand through my life and witness. Draw me close to Jesus so I can know Him better and represent Him in everything I say and do. Help me fan the flame of the Holy Spirit in my life. Amen.

Meditation: For this reason I remind you to fan into flame the gift of God, which is in you through the laying on of my hands. For the Spirit God gave us does not make us timid, but gives us power, love and self-discipline. (2 Timothy 1:6–7)

Worship: "Oceans" (Hillsong)

Tips: Quiet your spirit and invite the Holy Spirit's presence into you. A short prayer like, "come Holy Spirit, come" will help quiet your mind. Allow His calmness and grace to cover you before you do anything else. Now listen to His voice. Make sure you heed His warnings, confess what He asks you to confess, and do what He directs you to do according to His method and the time frame He desires.

I waited patiently for the LORD; he turned to me and heard my cry.

Psalm 40:1

THE TIME BETWEEN HARVEST AND SPRING

An Unexpected Ending Requires Faith

Harvest time in Champagne is one of the most exhilarating, as well as busiest, times of the year. All the hard work of tending the vines and waiting for the fruit to ripen while stressing over the weather, diseases, and insects has come to an end. Now you are able, literally, to reap your reward. Another successful year in Champagne is realized as the freshly plucked grapes are hauled inside the Champagne house to be pressed, fermented, and ultimately bottled, then corked and aged for everyone's enjoyment. For everyone's enjoyment, except one, the grape vines. The vines now begin the distressing journey to despair and barrenness. These once stately vines are now a series of branches, green leaves, and freshly cut stubs where magnificent grapes once hung ripening in the sunshine.

Soon the fall temperatures will turn these green leaves yellow then brown, and with the approach of winter they shrivel, detach, and are blown away. The green branches, once sprawling with life and vigor, start to harden and darken. Within six months, in the exact place where you once heard the joyful shouts of the harvesters, now hang, in the frigid and silent days of this season, barren and lifeless vines. The memories of a joyful life are now forgotten in these shorter and darker winter days. I am so glad that winter is followed by spring each year, aren't you?

Dark winter nights are not restricted to Champagne grape vines alone; they come unexpectedly, through the loving hands and will of our Father in heaven, into the lives of His children. In essence, we end up in Ezekiel's valley of bones not by anything we may have done wrong, but because our desire to know Him more and be more fruitful for Him requires long dark winter nights of the soul! Some might call it a crisis of faith, but in reality, it is the stripping away of the green of spring and summer and forcing you to make a decision in the dead solitude of winter regarding what you really believe about God. It is a place where God will reveal what is truly in your heart. Will you take God at His word, by faith, in the dead of winter when you see no evident signs of spring?

These are not glorious days, and sometimes the process might unfold over many months or several years. These are the days the leaves of an "untested" and "unexamined" faith dry up, fall off, and are blown away into the cold, dark night. The place where the green branches of a faith built on "good circumstances" now turn brown and harden with the cold reality of the solitude and silence of winter when life turns sour. This is the season for the removal of dross

(Proverbs 25:4) to get to a pure faith, which is more precious than gold (1 Peter 1:3–9). In winter, God strips you of everything you depended upon to give you comfort and identity until there is nothing left, and He remains silent to see how you will respond. Do you think God has your best in mind? Will you trust Him in the darkness? Will you surrender to His perfect will, though life seems unbearable right now? Or will you give up and let your confidence in God fade away into the wintry night?

It is so easy to lose your mind during these tumultuous days. Only through the kindness of friends and reminders from God that this long-lasting winter is for His glory will keep you from a pit of perpetual misery. Is there nothing that can be done?

Yes and no! We cannot rush the winter season; it is a fixed time determined by God alone. However, there is something we can do during these dark days. We can worship God and sing praises. In spite of the darkness, we praise Him. We praise Him by faith, not because of our circumstances. Until we are able to praise Him, thank Him, and sing songs of worship to Him in the deepest, darkest nights of our lives, our faith has not been fully refined by the cold of darkness and the silence of heaven.

It was by faith that Paul and Silas sang out to God while chained in the prisons of Philippi in the darkest and farthest part of the dungeon (see Acts 16:16–34 for the whole story). Having been whipped and flogged, they sang at midnight. And God caused an earthquake to shake their chains loose and open the doors. The result—God used that event to bring salvation to the jailer and his family.

It was also by faith that Jehoshaphat, facing an overwhelming military alliance of several nations (see 2 Chronicles 20 for the whole story), responded to God's call to not be afraid nor discouraged but march out and face the advancing army. As Jehoshaphat and his army went out to meet their foes, Jehoshaphat sent men in front of them to sing to and praise the Lord. And as they begin to worship, "the LORD set ambushes" (v. 22) against their enemies and defeated them (the opposing armies turned on each other and killed each other) and Israel carried off vast amounts of plunder without having to lift a sword in battle.

So sing! Sing! Sing praises to God in the darkness. Do not praise God with your eyes on your dark circumstances nor one eye on God and one eye on the winter night to see if your singing will set you free. Instead, focus your heart, mind, and both eyes, not on the darkness, but on the God who defeats mighty armies and sets prisoners free (Acts 12:1–19). His way of ending your winter and ushering you out of darkness into spring will never match your imagination of what you think you want and need. After all, His ways and thoughts are greater and more perfect than anything we can plan or create for ourselves (Isaiah 55:8–9).

So how can we look at the darkness and winter night when the greatest Light is shining before us? Paul and Silas were not expecting an earthquake to set their chains free, but they sang by faith. Jehoshaphat was not expecting God to set an ambush for his enemies, but he sent out men, by faith, in front of the army to sing. They sang to Him by faith in the darkest of times, and then God responded by doing only what God had imagined and planned to do in response to their act of faith in Him. So sing!

Father, I am distressed. I do not understand what is happening. Why are You so distant from me? Though I seek comfort, it eludes me. I long to hear Your voice but silence greets me instead. I find no relief and I seem to search and plead in vain. However, even though You do not speak to me, I will still worship You in my anguish. Father, show me why You have brought this season of darkness into my life and teach me to guard its lesson. Amen!

Meditation: I waited patiently for the Lord; he turned to me and heard my cry. He lifted me out of the slimy pit, out of the mud and mire; he set my feet on a rock and gave me a firm place to stand. He put a new song in my mouth, a hymn of praise to our God. Many will see and fear the Lord and put their trust in him. (Psalm 40:1–3)

Worship: "While I Wait" (Lincoln Brewster)

Tips: First, begin by worshiping and praising God. Second, acknowledge to God how miserable and unbearable these days are. Do not hold in your emotions. Instead express your emotions to God by praying the Psalms back to God (this is one of the many purposes the Psalms were given to us—for our benefit, growth, and comfort). Third, find a friend to confide in as you work through this dark time of your life. Finally, make sure to ask God why this season has come into your life. He will tell you when it's time for you to know.

*Yet to all who did receive him, to those who believed in his name,
he gave the right to become children of God.*

John 1:12

THE LABEL ON THE CHAMPAGNE BOTTLE

The Dry Bones of a False Identity

Next time you are in a wine shop, head over to the Champagne section and take some extra time to examine the labels on the bottles. You will notice several things of importance beginning with the name of the Champagne, perhaps Moët & Chandon. The location of the producer (for example, Epernay), will also be notated as well as the sweetness which is indicated as brut (dry), demi sec (slight to medium sweet), etc. The harvest year will be on the label if the Champagne is vintage: non-vintage Champagnes will not have a year notated. The alcohol content, as well as several other essential facts about the Champagne can also be found on its label. Of course, the most essential facts on the label are the two words, Champagne and France, the country of origin. These two words ensure you are purchasing a bottle of sparkling wine from the Champagne region

Paul's prayer for the Ephesians

For this reason I kneel before the Father, from whom every family in heaven and on earth derives its name. I pray that out of his glorious riches he may strengthen you with power through his Spirit in your inner being, so that Christ may dwell in your hearts through faith. And I pray that you, being rooted and established in love, may have power, together with all the Lord's holy people, to grasp how wide and long and high and deep is the love of Christ, and to know this love that surpasses knowledge—that you may be filled to the measure of all the fullness of God.

Now to him who is able to do immeasurably more than all we ask or imagine, according to his power that is at work within us, to him be glory in the church and in Christ Jesus throughout all generations, for ever and ever! Amen.

(Ephesians 3:14–21)

Meditation: Yet to all who received him, to those who believed in his name, he gave the right to become children of God—children born not of natural descent, nor of human decision or a husband's will, but born of God. (John 1:12–13)

Worship: "Who You Say I Am" (Hillsong)

Tips: Take time today to ponder how much you are loved and cared for by your heavenly Father. Think through all the ways He has watched over your life since you first came into this world. Now consider the false identities placed on you by yourself and others. Ask God if there are others you have forgotten about (He knows the whole list). As you pray, present these false identities to your Father, and allow Him to remove them one by one. Some labels are deeply entrenched in our minds. Keep going until you start experiencing the freedom of soaking in His love as a beloved daughter or son.

For he says, "In the time of my favor I heard you, and in the day of salvation I helped you." I tell you, now is the time of God's favor, now is the day of salvation.

2 Corinthians 6:2

THE URGENCY OF THE HARVEST

The Dry Bones of Missing God's Salvation

The harvest is the most anticipated event of the year in Champagne. There is a significant amount of work that leads up to the harvest in every vineyard. The decisions and preparations are enormous. Whether it is mending trellises, pruning and training the vines, cluster thinning, pest and disease control, or a host of other important tasks essential to producing a great crop of grapes, the vineyard operations are always ongoing as the focus of all this work is toward the harvest. With each passing day, as spring gives way to the warmer months of summer and then into fall, the grapes ripen until they reach perfection.

Once the grapes reach peak ripeness, the Champagne house begins in earnest to harvest future bottles of its finest Champagne over several weeks. It is the most urgent time of the year, and the window of opportunity is very short, so harvesters work extra hard during these days to gather the grapes. Of course, no one misses the harvest, for without the harvest there is no Champagne and everyone's work throughout the year would become pointless and wasted.

Tragically, while so many folks understand there are times in life of great urgency and seriousness, few take their eternal destination with such gravity. Ezekiel's valley is filled to overflowing with the dry bones of so many lost souls who have not treated the gospel of Christ with the same level of urgency as those in France do with the grape harvest each year in Champagne. The numbers are staggering of those who fritter away their lives missing the very purpose for which they were born into this world. The gospel is the most imperative of all messages we will ever hear in our lives. It compels us to decide this very moment in time, for it determines the eternal destination of every human being. It is a life-or-death choice. There is no greater choice than deciding what we believe about Jesus.

The gospel, which means good news, is not a complicated message that requires advanced degrees to understand its content. It does not require us to perform some heroic or generous act or deed to earn its rewards. The gospel is a gracious gift of salvation from a just and loving God to all people and is freely offered to all of us who wish to receive it (John 1:1–14; 3:16–21; 6:40).

The gospel message is this: we all need a Savior to wipe away our sins and rescue us from the coming wrath and justice of God against all sinners who refuse to repent of their sins. God has provided only one means of salvation to all human beings and that is through His Son, Jesus. It is through Jesus's death on the cross taking our place and the punishment for our sins that God offers us eternal peace with Him and the forgiveness of our sins. Though Jesus died on the cross and was buried in a tomb, He rose to life on the third day, confirming that His death is indeed sufficient to wash away our sins.

God's offer of salvation requires us to repent of our sins and receive Jesus as both our Savior and our Lord. At this point we become children of God and receive the Holy Spirit to live in us and help us live a new life worthy of Jesus. We are to be baptized to demonstrate to all that we now belong to Christ and Him alone. A new life with Jesus, with the help of the Holy Spirit, requires us to turn our backs on our old ways of living and focus our attention on knowing Jesus and doing His will in this world by doing good.

Now I know that some of you who are reading this will come to realize you need to choose God and make peace with Him this very moment. You are feeling convicted deep in your heart. You may have been resisting God for a long time or you have come to realize at this very instant that what you have always been searching for can only be found in Jesus. Maybe it has now become absolutely clear to you that your next step is to "Come to Jesus." If this is where your heart is right now and you have come to grips with your need of Christ as your Savior and are ready to begin a new life with Him, a simple prayer from your heart, letting Him know of your decision, is all that is required.

Jesus, I surrender my life to You today. Wash away my sins and make me new. I believe You died for me and were raised to life. You are now my Lord and my Savior. I wish to receive Your promised gift of the Holy Spirit. Help me know You better each day and live a life that is faithful to You. Show me the good You want

"So I say to you: Ask and it will be given to you; seek and you will find; knock and the door will be opened to you."

Luke 11:9

DAY 8

CHAMPAGNE UNDRUNK

The Dry Bones of Prayerlessness

Champagne should always be drunk immediately upon opening the bottle. Most people do. In fact, it would be quite odd for someone to open a bottle of Champagne and not immediately enjoy this magnificent drink. Champagne is at its pinnacle of effervescence and freshness as soon as the cork is removed. Pop, pour, toast, and drink. That is how Champagne works best. What does not work is pop, pour, toast, and wait. Unlike fine red wines that improve when exposed to air over a period of a few hours, waiting to drink an open bottle of Champagne will prove disappointing. The reason? All the CO_2, the source of the bubbles, dissipates leaving behind an austere, acidic, and very flat and uninspiring beverage.

Unfortunately, Champagne is not the only thing that loses its effervescence when not used promptly . . . our relationship with God goes very flat and unspectacular when we fail to pray. Prayerlessness is a serious issue for a disciple of Christ, because prayer is the means of communication and relationship with God. Prayer is the way we discern God's best path for our lives and the role we were made to play in His work of establishing His Kingdom on earth (Luke 11; Jeremiah 6:16; 1 Corinthians 12). Through prayer we receive His wisdom for each day to meet the challenges and opportunities He has set before us (Proverbs 8). Prayer is the place where we resolutely and with dogged determination surrender our imperfect will to His perfect will for our lives (Luke 11). Prayer is where unconfessed sins come to light and are repented of and forgiven (Luke 11). Prayer is where we can cry out in pain and distress seeking the "God of all comfort" to comfort us in our misery and know that the "Alpha and Omega" will comfort us when we pray (2 Corinthians 1, Revelation 1). It is through prayer we receive God's grace, kindness, and material needs in life when we ask Him (James 4). It is through prayer we find the things we lost, where we find the things God has prepared for us to enjoy in life and where we find the desires God has laid on our hearts when we seek Him (Luke 11). It is through prayer God opens great and mighty doors for us to go through that lead to opportunities to do "the work that God has prepared in advanced for us to do" (Ephesians 2:10) when we knock on His door (Luke 11). And it is through prayer where we ask God for His Holy Spirit, the infinite source of spiritual renewal, the infinite source of the bubbles in our lives, to fill us, empower us and send us out in the power, grace, and love of Christ to bring the effervescence and freshness of the gospel to a spiritually weary and thirsty world in need of something real to celebrate (Luke 11; Acts 1–2). In summary, prayer is the power behind every vibrant and healthy Christian life, but prayerlessness is the source of every unproductive, restless, and unspectacular Christian life.

In fact, prayerlessness was one of the causes of Israel's exile in Babylon in the 6th century BC, for they had ignored God's call to prayer (Jeremiah 35:17). Have you allowed God to show you your life of prayer as it currently exists? Perhaps we need God to show us the dry bones of prayerlessness in our own lives, for it can show up throughout the normal day. How many times have we gotten ourselves into avoidable trouble because we failed to pray? How many times have we missed God's best for our lives because we failed to pray? How many sleepless nights must we endure when peace is only a humbled saint on his or her knee seeking the loving Christ? How many relationships have been hurt because we failed to go before God in prayer on behalf of ourselves and the person we care about? Isn't it time to bring our dry bones of prayerlessness to God and ask Him to give them life? As James said, "the prayer of a righteous person is powerful and effective" (James 5:16). So let us pray.

Holy Spirit, breathe on the dry bones of my prayerless life. Revive the desire to pray and to seek my Father's face. Bring to mind the people and situations I need to be alert to and pray about this day. Open my heart to hear my Savior's voice and give me the courage to follow His voice wherever and to whomever He leads me toward today (John 10:1–18). Amen

Meditation: "So I say to you: Ask and it will be given to you; seek and you will find; knock and the door will be opened to you. For everyone who asks receives; the one who seeks finds; and to the one who knocks, the door will be opened." (Luke 11:9–10)

Worship: "Great Is Thy Faithfulness" (Chisholm/Runyan)

Tips: I highly commend *How to Pray* (R.A. Torrey) and *Prayer* (R. Foster) to help you develop a satisfying prayer life. Additionally, no prayer life would ever be complete without the Psalms. They are an inexhaustible trove that will enrich your heart, mind, and soul. The Psalms address our deepest emotions and all of life's circumstances, whether we are overflowing with joy or are in the depths of sorrow and depression. Select a psalm and pray it back to God, substituting your particular situation into the psalm. If you have never read the Psalms before, take a month to read all of them (there are 150 psalms, so only 5 per day).

Do not merely listen to the word, and so deceive yourselves.
Do what it says.

James 1:22

THE HOUSE STYLE

The Dry Bones of a Life that Doesn't Match One's Doctrine

The *Chef de Cave*, the cellar master or winemaker, is responsible for all the Champagne that comes out of the Champagne house, both vintage and non-vintage and ensuring that the non-vintage Champagne produced year after year reflects the house style that the Champagne house is noted for in the marketplace (all the characteristics including flavor, aroma, bubbles, texture). To create the house style, the Chef de Cave first combines still wines, called the *cuvée*, produced from multiple vineyards over several harvest seasons, into a base still wine which then undergoes the secondary bottle fermentation to produce the Champagne. The house champagne might be made from a blend of over seventy-five different still wines to produce the unique style, consistent year after year, that distinguishes that particular champagne house to the joy of its customers. Being consistent is essential at all Grande Marques—the greatest houses of Champagne—for the customers expect a consistent quality year after year considering the high prices paid for these great Champagnes. One thing for sure is that you will never find a lazy and careless Chef de Cave at any of these grand Champagne houses. Bringing disrepute and shame to one of these great names is a certain career-ender.

Consistency is not only expected by the customers of Champagne producers, it is also expected from our Lord in how we live our lives in light of His Word. To the extent our thoughts, words, and deeds do not line up with our Lord's precious teachings to us, we will find ourselves in limbo among the dry bones of Ezekiel's valley not able to go one way or the other until we address the inconsistencies in our lives. James, the brother of Jesus, reminds us,

> Do not merely listen to the word, and so deceive yourselves. Do what it says. Anyone who listens to the word but does not do what it says is like someone who looks at his face in a mirror and, after looking at himself, goes away and immediately forgets what he looks like. But whoever looks intently into the perfect law that gives freedom, and continues in it—not forgetting what they have heard, but doing it—they will be blessed in what they do. (James 1:22–25)

The world is watching us, or at least those in our immediate sphere of influence, and so our lack of compassionate deeds, hypocrisy, and compromises in light of sound doctrine are all grand paths leading to Ezekiel's valley of dry bones.

The Christian doctrine is powerful and transformative, and our lives should match its depth, richness, and vibrancy.

Why live an inconsistent life? We are to be the "salt of the earth" and not lose our saltiness (Matthew 5:13), bringing God's life into everything we do. It is only through our consistent actions and grace-filled speech that we win people to Christ.

Each day we are given the opportunity to spend time with our Lord in prayer and His Word, allowing Him to shape our lives in His image. Ask Him to show you all the inconsistencies in your life, both the things you are doing as well as not doing, and take the time to repent of them, one by one. He will forgive and restore you and move you out of Ezekiel's valley of dry bones and back upon the road He has called you to walk on with Him. We serve a joyful and loving God, so take the time to live a life that is authentic, a life that brings glory to Him. Live a life that captures the markings of the beauty, magnificence, and effervescence of the Christian doctrine and you will be a consistent and bright light (Matthew 5:14–16) to a world steeped in darkness.

Lord, through Your Holy Spirit, search my heart and my life for any words, thoughts and deeds that are inconsistent with Your perfect Word as revealed in Scripture. Also, show me the areas where I am lacking so I may become a mature follower of Christ (James 1:2–4). I ask for Your forgiveness in the following area _____ and I ask for Your help to mature me in this area of my life so that I may be dependable. Show me the steps necessary to repair any damage this may have caused. Thank You, Lord. Amen.

Meditation: But whoever looks intently into the perfect law that gives freedom, and continues in it—not forgetting what they have heard, but doing it—they will be blessed in what they do. (James 1:25)

Worship: "From the Inside Out" (Hillsong)

Tips: Practice contemplative Bible reading, also called *Lectio Divina*, on a regular basis. It is a simple technique for mediating on Scripture that enables the Holy Spirit to sift through your life and reveal truths that are most essential to your life at this moment. If this technique is new to you, ask your pastor, search the internet, or purchase a book on the subject. Once you start practicing contemplative Bible reading, you will soon find God identifying and removing the inconsistencies in your life, and your joy and peace will overflow as your life starts to match your doctrine.

us of the bubbles that should be in our lives are like a bad cork. Unfortunately, these sins are systemic and no human is without them. These public and private sins were the main cause of Israel's captivity in Babylon and the results of those sins were vividly illustrated in God's message to Ezekiel, "The hand of the LORD was on me, and he brought me out by the Spirit of the LORD and set me in the middle of a valley; it was full of bones. He led me back and forth among them, and I saw a great many bones on the floor of the valley, bones that were very dry" (Ezekiel 37:1–2).

Have you ever walked through your valley of dry bones of unconfessed and unrenounced sins? Have you ever allowed God to lead you "back and forth among" them? To allow His holy gaze and His Holy Word to point out the dry bones in your life and ask you "can these bones live?" There is no life in sin, only death reigns. God is not showing your sin to condemn you but to give you life. Do not wait another day but be quick to repent and confess your sins to God—"If we confess our sins, he is faithful and just and will forgive us our sins and purify us from all unrighteousness" (1 John 1:9)—and watch Him bring your dry bones to life.

Father, I confess the following to You _____ (put in the things you know right now). I repent of these things and I ask You to forgive me of my sin. Wash me in the blood of Jesus and make me as white as snow (Isaiah 1:18). Search my heart and my life for anything else I may have forgotten and make my sins "as far as the east is from the west" in your sight (Psalm 139:23–24; 103:11–12). Thank You, Father. Amen.

Meditation: If we confess our sins, he is faithful and just and will forgive us our sins and purify us from all unrighteousness. (1 John 1:9)

Worship: "Redeemer" (Nicole C. Mullen)

Tips: The absence of God's peace, contentment, and joy typically points to unconfessed sin in our lives. Pay attention to your reaction when you notice the sins others commit. The sins that bother us in others may likely be the very sin we are currently guilty of committing. Confession and turning away from them will lead to a clean heart and clear mind.

"... 'Master,' he said, 'you entrusted me with five talents. See, I have gained five more.'"

Matthew 25:20

THE AMAZING MADAME CLICQUOT (PART 1)

The Dry Bones of a Slothful Disciple

There is a lot of hard work that goes into the glass of Champagne we enjoy so much. We take for granted when we hold up our glass of Champagne to the light, we fully expect shimmering rays of light and sparkling bubbles and a clear glass of Champagne without any imperfection. In other words, we fully expect the Champagne house to filter out all the grape sediment (dead yeast and grape pieces) during the Champagne-making process, leaving behind an effervescent goblet of crystal-clear golden joy (or rose joy for those who are in the mood for pink Champagne). Fortunately, we have Madame Clicquot and her Chef de Cave, Antoine Muller, to thank for the clear

Champagne we drink today. Their innovative spirit and tenacity during the early parts of the 1800s created a process called *remuage* (riddling), which is a technique for gathering all the sediment at the neck of the bottle. The process has since been refined, perfected, and mechanized. Remuage was performed manually for almost two centuries and is still done by hand in some Champagne houses. Once remuage is complete, the sediment is disgorged in a swift and clean process leaving behind a clear, pristine beverage.

Her legacy of pursuing excellence in the quality of Champagne that bears her name is one of the two reasons (see Day 17) that Madame Clicquot's Veuve Clicquot Champagne is still one of the most respected brands in the industry today. After all, no one wants a cloudy glass of Champagne with chunks of grape and spent yeast floating around; we would all be better off with a glass of pure, clean water instead.

We should all stand in awe of what this amazing woman accomplished in pursuing excellence in Champagne making. She clearly did not squander the gift of owning a Champagne house by being content with the existing quality. Instead, she strived toward perfection, demanding the best of herself and others to produce the only quality that mattered in her eyes, "The Finest."

As followers of Christ, we too have gifts, bestowed upon us by the Third Person of the triune God, the Holy Spirit. These gifts are spiritual in nature, which are to be used to serve, expand, and build up our Lord's church, God's people (1 Corinthians 12–14). Everyone receives at least one spiritual gift from the Holy Spirit. Your church or pastor can help you discover and understand your spiritual gifting if you are uncertain what gifts you have received from the Holy Spirit. These are not our natural gifts and talents, but supernatural in nature, given to us to display God's work in this world through our lives (Ephesians 2:10) and assist our fellow believers in their devotion to Christ. God's kingdom and God's power are uniquely manifested through the exercise of these gifts. Only a disciple of Christ receives these supernatural gifts, and we can ask the Holy Spirit for additional spiritual gifts (1 Corinthians 12–14). Further, we are to develop these gifts through training and use so the quality of our service becomes in our Father's eyes, like Madame Cliquot's champagne, "The Finest."

Notice that these spiritual gifts were not given to us by the Holy Spirit for our own pleasure, to be developed at our convenience nor to be used at our leisure. They are ultimately given to manifest the magnificence and glory of Jesus and display His love in this world to others. It is easy to give in to our own lack of discipline and not put forth the concerted effort required to identify and develop our spiritual gifts. In essence, we choose a comfortable spot to lie down among the dry bones instead of discovering, embracing, and putting to work the great treasures the Lord has entrusted to us.

The expansion of God's kingdom through our lives is not possible if we remain slothful toward developing our spiritual gifts. A sense of restlessness in our Christian faith may be a sign that we have allowed our own neglect to drag us into Ezekiel's valley. Leaving that valley of dry bones is a decision. It requires a resolute spirit that pushes forward despite our own inertia. It requires us to stop and listen to our Lord (Luke 10:38–42) and focus on doing whatever He requires. In short, we need to surrender our will and reprioritize our lives around Him.

So let us not squander the grace God has given us and waste the immense and precious gifts we have received. Instead, with the Holy Spirit's help, we will commit to diligently put forth the effort to fully understand and develop

Therefore put on the full armor of God, so that when the day of evil comes, you may be able to stand your ground, and after you have done everything, to stand.

Ephesians 6:13

THE VINEYARD MANAGER

The Dry Bones of Surrendering to the Enemy

The vineyard manager or head viticulturist of a Champagne house is responsible for overseeing the entire vineyard's operations. There are new vines to plant, canopy management strategies and pruning schedules to determine, vine production records to maintain, and of course the supervising of the harvest. Additionally, the vineyard manager has employees to supervise and train, as well as budgets to be planned and to be kept. There is a lot of pressure on the head viticulturist at a Champagne house to ensure the vineyard runs well.

Of course, one of the most critical elements is monitoring the health of the grapes and vines. You see, there are a lot of potential threats and enemies to the grapes and vines: blight, disease, insects, birds, wild animals, and bad weather. A good vineyard manager will be alert to these dangers and take precautions to prevent these things from interfering with the vineyard. In the event these enemies happen to show up, the vineyard manager has ways to quickly identify attacks and take corrective actions before things get too far out of hand. It is easier to deal with a minor annoyance now than try to eradicate a major problem left unattended. One thing the vineyard manager will not do however is surrender the grapes and vines to the whims of these destroyers without putting up a vicious and protracted fight to rescue the precious grape harvest and prevent the ruin of these valuable vines. After all, bottles of Champagne are at stake.

I believe a toast is in order, with the finest of bubbly, to every vineyard manager in Champagne. They have trained hard, prepared wisely, and armed themselves with the latest viticulture tools of the trade to handle every enemy that seeks to destroy and cause havoc to the grape crops. Cheer!! Cheer!! If only the same could be said for every follower of Jesus when "the great dragon . . . that ancient serpent called the devil, or Satan, who leads the whole world astray" (Revelation 12:9), strikes. Unfortunately, if we are not adequately prepared for the devil's schemes against us (Ephesians 6:10–20), we will surrender some area of our lives to Satan and quickly find ourselves in the valley of dry bones because we put up the white flag and allowed Satan a foothold into our lives (Ephesians 4:27).

He is our enemy! Satan is not to be obeyed, negotiated with, or even have any of his opinions considered. Jesus described him as a thief who "comes only to steal and kill and destroy" (John 10:10). He is a liar (John 8:44)! Peter described him as a "roaring lion looking for someone to devour" (1 Peter 5:8). Does that sound like someone who has your best interest at heart?

Satan also "masquerades as an angel of light" (2 Corinthians 11:14); he tries to hide his true intentions and deceive us by making something seem right and good, even though upon closer examination we see it as destructive to us and those closest to us. Satan's schemes are revealed to us through God's Word, the Holy Spirit, and even the counsel of godly friends. He even went after Jesus on multiple occasions (Matthew 4; John 8:44; Matthew 16:23) and eventually entered Judas who then proceeded to betray Jesus to His executioners.

Satan hates every disciple of Christ and actively tempts us to violate or ignore the commands and will of God (Genesis 3; 1 Thessalonians 3:5). He works hard at trying to keep our eyes off Jesus by sowing problems, enemies (even in our own households; Matthew 10:34–36), fear, intimidation, anxiety, and stress into our lives. His fruit is anger, bitterness, resentment, chaos, division, disharmony, slander, pride, misunderstandings, self-condemnation, selfishness, hopelessness, and everything contrary to God's perfect Word (Galatians 5:19–21; Romans 1:18–32). He even tempts us to doubt God's goodness and love toward us (Genesis 3). If we are not "alert and of sober mind" (1 Peter 5:8) and ready to identify and face these attacks, we are going to get distracted from our Lord and His work of redemption and renewal in this world. We could potentially bring shame to Him if we give in to Satan's will.

If we find ourselves having surrendered some area of our lives to Satan as a result of an attack, the first order of business is to turn back to God, repent of our errors, and surrender that area of life to Him. God loves us and will immediately forgive, restore, and strengthen us. The next step is to "stand firm in the faith" and resist Satan, using the spiritual armor God has provided to us, which includes the Word of God as our weapon against him (1 Peter 5:9; James 4:7; Ephesians 6:10–20). The spiritual battle may be rough and long, but the Bible promises that Satan will flee

(James 4:7). Remember that Christ has defeated Satan on your behalf through His victory on the cross and resurrection from the grave (Colossians 2:13–15). So "be strong in the Lord and his mighty power" and "take your stand against the devil's schemes" (Ephesians 6:10–11), and remember "the one who is in you is greater than the one who is in the world" (1 John 4:4).

The power and light shining brightly from the Holy Spirit in your life is enough to snuff out all the darkness Satan can conjure up against you. Stand firm on the gospel that saved you and do not shrink back (Hebrews 10:32–39; Revelation 12:11). The kingdom of God is not for the timid soul (Matthew 11:12), for we have been given the power to demolish spiritual strongholds (2 Corinthians 10:3–5) and bind or cast out Satan by the authority of the name of Jesus (Matthew 16:19; 18:18–20; Luke 11:17–22). Remember Jesus's words to His disciples: "Do not be afraid, little flock, for your Father has been pleased to give you the kingdom" (Luke 12:32). And again: "On this rock I will build my church, and the gates of Hades will not overcome it" (Matthew 16:18). So do not surrender anything to the enemy, but "be strong and courageous. Do not be afraid; do not be discouraged" (Joshua 1:9) and focus your heart, mind, and all your energy on Jesus and His work for you today.

Turn Your Eyes Upon Jesus (Helen H. Lemmel)

O soul, are you weary and troubled?
No light in the darkness you see?
There's light for a look at the Savior,
And life more abundant and free.

Turn your eyes upon Jesus,
Look full in His wonderful face,
And the things of earth will grow strangely dim,
In the light of His glory and grace.

Through death into life everlasting
He passed, and we follow Him there;
O'er us sin no more hath dominion
For more than conqu'rors we are!

Turn your eyes upon Jesus,
Look full in His wonderful face,
And the things of earth will grow strangely dim,
In the light of His glory and grace.

His Word shall not fail you, He promised;
Believe Him and all will be well;
Then go to a world that is dying,
His perfect salvation to tell!

Turn your eyes upon Jesus,
Look full in His wonderful face,
And the things of earth will grow strangely dim,
In the light of His glory and grace.

Meditation: Therefore put on the full armor of God, so that when the day of evil comes, you may be able to stand your ground, and after you have done everything, to stand. (Ephesians 6:13)

Worship: "Turn Your Eyes Upon Jesus" (Helen H. Lemmel)

Tips: There is no such thing as a spiritual holiday when it comes to the devil's schemes. He is always looking for a kink in our spiritual armor and is ready to pounce as soon as we drop our guard. His goal is to destroy us! Memorizing and praying Ephesians 6:13–18 is a good strategy. Unless we prepare for the battle each day, we will struggle more than we need and put ourselves into a position of failure instead of success when a spiritual attack comes our way. Accomplishing God's purpose for our lives requires His armor. So, suit up!

A little while, and the wicked will be no more;
though you look for them, they will not be found.
But the meek will inherit the land
and enjoy peace and prosperity.

Psalm 37:10–11

AGING CHAMPAGNE

The Dry Bones of Fretting over Wicked People

By French law, Champagnes must be aged a minimum number of years before they are released to the public. Fifteen months is the minimum timeframe for non-vintage Champagne and three years for vintage. In practice, the major Champagne houses will age their Champagnes significantly longer prior to release. You may wonder why there is such a long aging process. The reason is that young Champagnes are naturally harsh and acidic, lacking the flavor profile of that house and unfit for drinking young. The aging process mellows out the harshness and acidity and allows the unique flavor profile of that house to develop into all its fullness. In fact, Champagnes can be aged even longer by the consumer allowing the Champagnes to develop even more character and complexity to the delight of their owners. The reality is that some glorious and spectacular things require you to wait patiently to experience joy in all its fullness instead of rushing ahead impatiently and reaping an unpleasant and lingering tartness in your mouth as a reward for your haste.

Harshness and acidity are not only issues for Champagne, they are also issues for every follower of Christ when it comes to our attitudes and responses when dealing with wicked people. These are the people who pervert the ways of God and trample on all we cherish and hold dear. The things of God are foolishness to those who do not know Him, so they do not believe in absolute moral standards. What was once thought inconceivable by any society to embrace has now become the norm with little thought that there is a day of accountability to our Creator (Romans 1:18–21).

When it comes to all the wickedness you see and experience each day, how do you respond? Do you find yourself upset and angry? Do you struggle with a judgmental and condemning attitude? Unfortunately, if we do not have a biblical perspective of the future of the wicked, we can find ourselves buried today among the dry bones because we are fretting over the wicked. God's counsel for us today is found in Psalm 37:

> Be still before the LORD
>   and wait patiently for him;
> do not fret when people succeed in their ways,
>   when they carry out their wicked schemes.
> Refrain from anger and turn from wrath;
>   do not fret—it leads only to evil.
> For those who are evil will be destroyed,
>   but those who hope in the LORD will inherit
>   the land.
> A little while, and the wicked will be no more;
>   though you look for them, they will not be
>   found.
> But the meek will inherit the land
>   and enjoy peace and prosperity.

(Psalm 37:7–11)

The answer to our dry bones is to apply a similar "aging" process to the wicked as to Champagne. We do this by showing them love, caring for their needs, and praying for their eternal salvation so that in time the harshness and acidity may be overcome by the radiant and overwhelming love of Christ shining through our lives (Matthew 5:43–48). It was not so long ago that we too were alienated from God and He showed us kindness through someone in our lives turning us from death to life, from falsehood to truth, and from being a rebel to being God's friend. Therefore, spend no more of your life fretting over the actions of those who live without any future hope (Proverbs 24:19–20), but instead love them as your Savior loves you.

Father, change my heart and my perspective toward all people so that my life conforms to Your heart and Your perspective (Romans 12:9–21):

Love must be sincere. Hate what is evil; cling to what is good. Be devoted to one another in love. Honor one another above yourselves. Never be lacking in zeal, but keep your spiritual fervor, serving the Lord. Be joyful in hope, patient in affliction, faithful in prayer. Share with the Lord's people who are in need. Practice hospitality.

Bless those who persecute you; bless and do not curse. Rejoice with those who rejoice; mourn with those who mourn. Live in harmony with one another. Do not be proud, but be willing to associate with people of low position. Do not be conceited.

Do not repay anyone evil for evil. Be careful to do what is right in the eyes of everyone. If it is possible, as far as it depends on you, live at peace with everyone. Do not take revenge, my dear friends, but leave room for God's wrath, for it is written: "It is mine to avenge; I will repay," says the Lord. On the contrary:

> *"If your enemy is hungry, feed him;*
>   *if he is thirsty, give him something to drink.*
> *In doing this, you will heap burning coals on his head."*

Do not be overcome by evil, but overcome evil with good. Amen!

Meditation: Be still before the LORD and wait patiently for him; do not fret when people succeed in their ways, when they carry out their wicked schemes. Refrain from anger and turn from wrath; do not fret—it leads only to evil. For those who are evil will be destroyed, but those who hope in the LORD will inherit the land. (Psalm 37:7–9)

Worship: "A Mighty Fortress Is Our God" (Luther)

Tips: The words and actions of wicked people can make us feel anxious, powerless, and frightened! This is especially true if they have the ability to impact our lives. Resist the temptation to lash out or run away (unless in danger). Our job is to stand firm for the gospel. God will watch over our lives. Turn your heart to your Father for comfort! Philippians 4:4–7 (memorize) tells us not to be anxious, but to rejoice in the Lord, be gentle, and pray with a thankful heart. Those who follow these instructions will experience the supernatural peace of God regardless of what the wicked do or say.

Now searching out and investing in old, prestigious bottles of Champagne may not be your thing nor fit within your limited financial means, but there is one treasure which God directs all of us to seek out and invest in daily: His Kingdom. "Do not store up for yourselves treasures on earth, where moths and vermin destroy, and where thieves break in and steal. But store up for yourselves treasures in heaven, where moths and vermin do not destroy, and where thieves do not break in and steal" (Matthew 6:19–20). Our Lord is pointing us to the greatest possible use of our earthly resources. Yet, because of our own fears, pride, or desire for pleasure, comfort, and security, we ignore His leading. We may either put forth a partial effort or neglect the command entirely. We assume it is an unreasonable request given our current financial goals or situation.

You see, kingdom treasures do not appeal to our physical and psychological senses, but to faith in what God has in store for us and others. They are unseen and compete for our attention with the strong pull of the here and now of earthly treasure. The sirens of earthly gold sing a most alluring and beautiful melody but take one look at the shipwrecked souls in Ezekiel's valley of dry bones and we will wish we had plugged our ears and closed our eyes. Safe passage through these treacherous waters requires us to navigate one obstacle, the condition and focus of our hearts. "For where your treasure is, there your heart will be also" (Matthew 6:21).

Our hearts will never find contentment when we allow earthly desires to displace our affection for God. The challenge we face is whether we have a heart that trusts God with our tomorrows and is aligned with God's plans for this very day. It does not mean we deprive ourselves of good things, rather we carefully consider whether the lifestyle we are maintaining is contributing to God's kingdom. Are our lifestyles pointing others to Christ or robbing God of what is rightfully His, causing us to forfeit opportunities to invest in treasures that endure for all of eternity? We should all consider the gravity of the choice laid before us considering this parable told by Jesus:

> Someone in the crowd said to him, "Teacher, tell my brother to divide the inheritance with me." Jesus replied, "Man, who appointed me a judge or an arbiter between you?" Then he said to them, "Watch out! Be on your guard against all kinds of greed; life does not consist in an abundance of possessions." And he told them this parable: "The ground of a certain rich man yielded an abundant harvest. He thought to himself, 'What shall I do? I have no place to store my crops.' "Then he said, 'This is what I'll do. I will tear down my barns and build bigger ones, and there I will store my surplus grain. And I'll say to myself, "You have plenty of grain laid up for many years. Take life easy; eat, drink and be merry."' "But God said to him, 'You fool! This very night your life will be demanded from you. Then who will get what you have prepared for yourself?' "This is how it will be with whoever stores up things for themselves but is not rich toward God." (Luke 12:13–21)

Investing our wealth in earthly treasures will only yield an impoverished heart. However, if we spend our lives storing up "treasures in heaven" we will enjoy a rich and warm-hearted spirit while on earth.

Pray for a heart that embraces all the possibilities envisioned by Jesus when He taught about real treasure:

"The kingdom of heaven is like treasure hidden in a field. When a man found it, he hid it again, and then in his joy went and sold all he had and bought that field. Again, the kingdom of heaven is like a merchant looking for fine pearls. When he found one of great value, he went away and sold everything he had and bought it." (Matthew 13:44–46)

Meditation: "Do not store up for yourselves treasures on earth, where moths and vermin destroy, and where thieves break in and steal. But store up for yourselves treasures in heaven, where moths and vermin do not destroy, and where thieves do not break in and steal. For where your treasure is, there your heart will be also." (Matthew 6:19–21)

Worship Song: "Be Thou My Vision" (Ancient Irish Hymn)

Tips: The vaults of heaven are always open for deposits: (1) It is better to concentrate your energy and resources into a few things than many; and (2) God will send people into your life who need to experience His provision. So be ready and be generous. You never know how one unexpected act of kindness will transform the rest of that person's life. You may literally be their last hope before they do something tragic, not knowing how to get out of the current situation.

"*This is to my Father's glory, that you bear much fruit, showing yourselves to be my disciples.*"

John 15:8

DAY 16

IN THE SHADOWS OF THE GREAT CHAMPAGNE HOUSES

The Dry Bones of Seeking Your Own Glory

Behind every great Champagne house are hundreds or thousands of ordinary workers who form the backbone of the organization and bear the heat of the day to keep the house running smoothly. These are the employees responsible for tending the vineyards, the scientists in the lab, the facility cleaning crews, the production team, the *remueurs*, the finance department, and every other non-senior level executive position at the Champagne house. It is unlikely you will read about them in trade magazines or featured on TV or in newspapers. Media's spotlight shines on the Champagne house itself and the major movers and shakers of the industry, not on the little guy or gal.

Hopefully those who hold a lower-level position are thankful they work in the shadows of one of these great names of Champagne and are content with their lot in life. On the other hand, if someone was trying to carve out a name for themselves, they might find life very disappointing when the rewards, recognition, and glory they yearned for never fully materialize to meet their expectations or eludes them altogether. Sometimes it is better to be thankful for the privilege to work at one of these Champagne houses, even if it is in the shadows.

Seeking our own glory, whether deliberately or subconsciously, is a hollow pursuit and will ultimately prove unsatisfying and disappointing. It also happens to be one of the quickest detours to Ezekiel's valley of dry bones, far from the warmth and joy of the presence of our heavenly Father. It is easy to fool ourselves into thinking our motivations are pure when in fact our desire for praise and recognition is deeply interwoven into our actions and hearts. How we respond when people do not acknowledge our efforts will quickly show us what is truly driving our actions. Do we feel that others should be more grateful and appreciative of our hard work, thoughtfulness, and dedication? Do we get discouraged and feel slighted when those who do not put in the effort are dismissive or critical? Or do we still maintain our joy and contentment regardless of how others react?

Consider the people, things, and activities (such as school or work) that you have poured out your heart, strength, wisdom, and energy into over many years. What was your motivation? Was it to bring glory to Jesus (Colossians 3:17)? Did you work at it with the strength that God provided to you (Philippians 4:12–13; Isaiah 40:29–31)? Did you ask God for the wisdom in how to undertake your responsibilities (James 1:5–8)? Did you listen to Him as He guided you along over the years (James 1:22–25)? Or was it all for your own renown and praise?

The only way out of Ezekiel's valley of dry bones is to put aside your need for glory and commit yourself to work in the shadows of the Savior, "whatever you do, work at it with all your heart, as working for the Lord, not for human masters, since you know that you will receive an inheritance from the Lord as a reward. It is the Lord Christ you are serving" (Colossians 3:23–24). See also Ephesians 6:7–8. When you lay down your need for glory and recognition and are ready to do what Jesus commands— serving those He brings into your life—you will experience a freedom from the need for human praise and will enjoy instead the pleasure of our Lord.

Father, forgive me for seeking my own glory in the following matter _____. I lay down my need for praise and recognition from people, even from those closest to me (family, friends, and coworkers). Instead, I desire to submit to Your good and perfect will regarding this matter. Refocus my attention on how I can please You and bear much fruit, for Your glory. Amen.

Meditation: "If you remain in me and my words remain in you, ask whatever you wish, and it will be done for you. This is to my Father's glory, that you bear much fruit, showing yourselves to be my disciples." (John 15:7–8)

Worship: "Revelation Song" (Phillips, Craig, and Dean)

Tips: Anytime you interact with someone is an opportunity to allow the glory of God to shine through your life. Prior to saying a word, begin with prayer, "Lord, give me words to speak and guide my actions so they hear Your voice and experience Your presence and not me." Now listen and allow yourself to be led by the Holy Spirit. Though you may not see immediate results, you can be sure your Father will work mightily through your life and into the life of the other person. Make sure you thank your Father for the opportunity and ask Him to cause your words and actions to bear fruit in that other person's life. A pattern of prayer throughout the day will keep you alert for opportunities God brings your way.

"From everyone who has been given much, much will be demanded; and from the one who has been entrusted with much, much more will be asked."

Luke 12:48b

THE AMAZING MADAME CLICQUOT (PART 2)

The Dry Bones of Neglecting Your Assignment

With the tragic death of her husband in 1805, Madame Clicquot was left, at age twenty-seven, with a daughter, a Champagne house, and an uncertain future. Persuading her father-in-law to allow her to run the Champagne house, she agreed to his stipulation that she undertake an apprenticeship to prove she was capable to meet the challenge and responsibility of running the family business. It was not the life she had hoped for apart from her husband, but with vigorous hands and an unbendable spirit for making the best champagne, she built something that has now lasted over 200 years. Madame Clicquot possessed entrepreneurial zeal and a willingness to make personal sacrifices. She had the determination to take advantage of every opportunity presented her way, which helped her navigate the financial, social, and competitive turmoil and challenges of her day to realize great success. In an industry dominated by men, she became known as the Grande Dame of Champagne, held in great esteem by her industry peers.

Considering what she accomplished, it is hard to imagine that Veuve Clicquot (*Veuve* means widow) might have never existed if she had chosen the dark shadows of fear and bitter heartache to rule her life in 1805. She could have distracted herself with inconsequential pursuits that offered no risk of crushed hopes, but would be void of life and meaning. She could have succumbed to social standards of the day and not approached her father-in-law for the opportunity to run the Champagne house. Instead, within a few years this audacious woman would affix Veuve to the Champagne house that bears her name and press forward with deep conviction that this was her life's assignment, not to be neglected for any reason.

Fear, bitter heartaches, frivolous distractions, and other people's expectations and priorities are some of the many names written on the dry bones scattered along Ezekiel's valley that we may find ourselves shuffling along. They are the tombstones that will mark the graveyard of our lives when we allow them sovereignty over our hearts instead of our Lord and His work for us in this world. Jesus was emphatic in His expectations that to be His disciple was to be fully engaged in the work He has assigned to each of us:

> The Lord answered, "Who then is the faithful and wise manager, whom the master puts in charge of his servants to give them their food allowance at the proper time? It will be good for that servant whom the master finds doing so when

he returns. Truly I tell you, he will put him in charge of all his possessions. But suppose the servant says to himself, 'My master is taking a long time in coming,' and he then begins to beat the other servants, both men and women, and to eat and drink and get drunk. The master of that servant will come on a day when he does not expect him and at an hour he is not aware of. He will cut him to pieces and assign him a place with the unbelievers." (Luke 12:42–46)

This was not the only time Jesus spoke about the importance of being about His business and not neglecting our assignments. He used illustrations involving bags of gold (Matthew 25:14–30), grape vines (John 15:1–17), and the cross (Mark 8:34–37) to drive home the point that His work is serious, of first priority, and not optional. Neglecting our assignment will result in us missing a fruitful life while on earth and will ultimately have eternal consequences.

Look, the disciple of Christ will always encounter treacherous landscapes that cause fainter hearts to tremble but move forward regardless because our Lord beckons us on. Pursuing inconsequential and lesser distractions will always be a temptation. However, we are God's children. Our Father has given us the Holy Spirit. Our Lord has laid down His life for our salvation. We have God's Word and all His promises at our disposal. We can have anything we ask for in prayer that is aligned with God's will, and God has told us He wants His will done.

Therefore, we need to let go of the past, the hurts, and whatever is hindering us from the Lord's call on our lives and embrace our Savior and the adventure before us. The finish line is so close we can taste it. Even those of us who are tired, and our energy is spent, keep moving forward because with each step the Lord will add something new and bring things into better focus.

Remember, if Madame Clicquot had neglected such a great and mighty door that was opened before her, even amid hardships and deep hurts, she would have missed her life and deprived us all of her effervescent and richly textured creation. How much more so for a disciple of Christ? We must take care of what God has given us, otherwise we end up losing it for ourselves and also for future generations. Finally, remember the admonishment of our Savior, "From everyone who has been given much, much will be demanded; and from the one who has been entrusted with much, much more will be asked" (Luke 12:48b). So get busy!

Lord, forgive me for allowing fear, bitter heartaches, frivolous distractions, other people's expectations and priorities, and _____ to distract me from You and the work You have given me to do in this world. Forgive me for asking for new assignments when I have left other things undone. Please refocus my attention on You and help me no longer stray from Your path but do the work You have made for me to do (Ephesians 2:10). Lord, I claim the promise that when I am faithful in the work You have given me You will also give me more (Luke 12:44). Jesus, I am now in agreement with the apostle Paul's words, "I was not disobedient to the vision from heaven" (Acts 26:19) and with Your help I want to live a life of wondrous obedience to the great call that You have on my life. Amen.

Meditation: "From everyone who has been given much, much will be demanded; and from the one who has been entrusted with much, much more will be asked." (Luke 12:48b)

Worship: "So Will I" (Hillsong)

Tips: Beware of the slippage of time and be intentional about Jesus and the work that He would have you do in this world! Weeks will slip into years if we are negligent, and we will look back with regret that we didn't give our best for Jesus. Don't miss out on the life He wants for you. Go back to the last assignment He gave you and work diligently to complete that good work. If you need an assignment, ask Him for one! Set aside the necessary time to work on it until you are done. He will help you complete His work. Once you are about your assignment you will quickly notice that your life will become vibrant, purposeful, productive, and meaningful as you invest your life in God's work.

Praise be to the God and Father of our Lord Jesus Christ, the Father of compassion and the God of all comfort, who comforts us in all our troubles, so that we can comfort those in any trouble with the comfort we ourselves receive from God.

2 Corinthians 1:3–4

AN UNTRELLISED VINE

The Dry Bones of Failing to Lighten the Burdens of Others

Vines require cultivation to produce the grapes that are worthy to produce the finest Champagne. One of the keys to the successful cultivation of grape vines is the use of trellises. The trellising system is used to optimize sun exposure, reduce the risk of loss to insects and diseases, improve the efficiency of pruning and harvesting, and ultimately maximize the quality and quantity of the grapes. The trellising system is essential as grape vines by nature are not strong enough to bear the weight of their branches and the clusters of grapes and thus require support. Apart from something holding them up, the clusters of beautiful grapes will rest on the ground subject to crawling insects, hungry passing animals, mold, and eventual rot. This is not a very good way to run a Champagne house. Thank goodness for trellises to lighten the burden of the grape vines. Great Champagne would not be possible without them.

Trellises are not only designed to hold up vines, but they are also designed to hold up people. These trellises are not made of wire but made of flesh and blood. We live in a world where people carry burdens too heavy to bear on their own. These are the type of burdens that weigh down the soul in dread and darkness. Names of those you know who are carrying burdens may come immediately to mind. They are dearly loved family members or friends, neighbors and coworkers, as well as those we have seen on television or read about. Each one of them is in desperate need of a kind heart to comfort and care for them. In fact, at some point in our lives we will carry a burden too heavy to carry on our own.

Whatever their burden, those who find ways to lighten it are the most prized and precious people in the world. Sadly, in reading this we may realize we have been so consumed with our own lives that we have ignored or been oblivious to the emotional weight others carry all around us. Worse, we may realize that we have added on to the burdens of others instead of taking the load off. If this is the case, the best course of action is to weep and allow our hearts to grieve among the valley of dry bones, for these bones are the burdens of others too heavy for them to lift alone.

It is at this point we can hear with tender ears the words from the apostle Paul in his letter to the Corinthian church, "Praise be to the God and Father of our Lord Jesus Christ, the Father of compassion and the God of all comfort, who comforts us in all our troubles, so that we can comfort those in any trouble with the comfort we ourselves receive from God" (2 Corinthians 1:3–4). We should take time to walk around Ezekiel's valley and be filled with compassion for those suffering all around us. Let the calloused portions of our love soften to the distressed plight of others. Ask our

Lord to give us renewed and sensitive hearts so we can follow the Holy Spirit's leading and notice others who need a friend to come alongside them during difficulty.

Maybe *we* are the ones carrying the heavy weight and therefore think we are in no position to assist someone else. Actually, we are the best ones to help because we know what it means to bear a burden. People want someone who has traveled into the dark abyss of life's crushing blows and emerged with hope and joy. They want someone who can describe their pain with all its raw emotion.

So, what do we do to help? First, remember Jesus is the one who carries our sorrows and our burdens (Isaiah 53:4; Matthew 11:28–30). Let Him carry the weight of your burden. Second, look around and be alert to others around you. Do not ignore your own family in the process. Just be ready and willing to help. Finally, when given an opportunity, ask Jesus for a specific way you can help lift even a little bit of that person's burden. You do not need to carry the whole thing, but an act of generosity, a warm meal, or even a hug will lighten one's heart.

Remember, a trellis is designed to carry weight and allow whatever it bears to develop into its full potential. Likewise, take time to lighten the burden of others and point them to the One who loves you and bears your burdens so they may experience the fullness of the love of Christ in their desperate situation through your actions. Also, remember the words of Jesus directed to His servants who lightened the burdens of others,

> "Then the King will say to those on his right, 'Come, you who are blessed by my Father, take your inheritance, the kingdom prepared for you since the creation of the world. For I was hungry and you gave me something to eat, I was thirsty

and you gave me something to drink, I was a stranger and you invited me in, I needed clothes and you clothed me, I was sick and you looked after me, I was in prison and you came to visit me.'" (Matthew 25:34–36)

Father, open opportunities for me to lighten other people's burdens. Forgive me for being so concerned about my own life that I am not focusing on those around me. Give me a tender heart toward others and help me demonstrate Your love for them in practical ways. For any burdens I am holding onto, I now release them into Your loving hands and help me to receive Your comfort from those You send my way. Amen.

Meditation: "Then the King will say to those on his right, 'Come, you who are blessed by my Father, take your inheritance, the kingdom prepared for you since the creation of the world. For I was hungry and you gave me something to eat, I was thirsty and you gave me something to drink, I was a stranger and you invited me in, I needed clothes and you clothed me, I was sick and you looked after me, I was in prison and you came to visit me.'" (Matthew 25:34–36)

Worship: "Shadow Step" (Hillsong)

Tips: Offer a listening ear to someone who is grieving (Romans 12:15). Clean the house of a friend who is going through a divorce. Bring flowers or a meal to a family who has lost a loved one. Be kind to the unemployed. For those who recently lost a beloved pet, order a picture frame with the pet's name engraved. An encouraging and kind word lets someone know they are valued. Give someone a long hug!

I want to know Christ—yes, to know the power of his resurrection and participation in his sufferings, becoming like him in his death, and so, somehow, attaining to the resurrection from the dead.

Philippians 3:10–11

DAY 19

CHAMPAGNE OR CRÉMANT?

The Dry Bones of Competing First Loves

Crémant is the name for sparkling wines from France produced with the same production method employed by Champagne producers. This method is called the traditional method; referred to as *méthode champenoise* by Champagne producers. The notable thing about the traditional method is the second fermentation takes place in the bottle. This adds a unique, rich flavor profile and aroma to the wine called autolytic character (bread/biscuit/nuttiness; typically these flavors and aromas are more pronounced with longer aging cycles in the cellar). Crémant are excellent sparkling wines and well worth serving at any festive gathering or to enjoy during a quiet evening after work. They tend to be very reasonably priced and are easy on your budget. Though these wines have much going for them, there is, however, one catch . . . Crémant is not from the Champagne region. It is made using grapes grown outside the borders of Champagne and thus can never be called Champagne. In addition, the majority of Crémants do not undergo the same rigorous production standards common among Champagne producers (such as longer aging on lees, the accumulated sediment from the fermentation process) that result in the characteristic elegant tiny bubbles, as well as the complexity of flavors and aromas that makes Champagne unique and famous among sparkling wines.

Now I know Crémants have a close resemblance and substitutability to Champagne, but they are not Champagne. They are delicious, but they can never match the quality, the magnificence, the prestige, the heritage, the beauty, and the worth of Champagne. When life requires the best in sparkling wines, resist the temptation of an inexpensive and unmemorable substitute. Let it go and instead embrace the one whose vines grow in the choicest and hallowed of all soils, Champagne.

Letting go of a bottle of Crémant when the alternative is Dom Pérignon is not especially hard to do, provided you are willing to absorb the substantial cost difference. It is not so easy when faced with a decision not involving our choice of sparkling wine but our Christian faith, when our decision to follow Christ starts to attract opposition. When choosing an alternative route, while relieving the immediate pain, is paramount to the betrayal of our Lord. Under such circumstances, we can inadvertently become thrust into Ezekiel's valley of dry bones and find ourselves torn between our first love for the Lord and pleasing the desires of others who are competing with Him for our undivided affections and loyalty.

This issue is most apparent if we are driven by the fear of people and being acceptable in their eyes. We fear the loss we might suffer if we choose the Lord's will over their will. The fear is especially acute if we might lose a close relationship, our position at work, or our reputation in the eyes of others. Being aligned with Jesus is costly. The more substantial the person's influence over our lives, the greater the temptation to appease them at the cost of our intimacy with Christ.

When we succumb to the will of people, we will find our peace taken away, the joy of the Lord missing, and our once sure foundation replaced with doubt and uncertainty about how to proceed in life.

What are we to do? In Paul's letter to the church in Philippi we find an answer to our dilemma, "I want to know Christ—yes, to know the power of his resurrection and participation in his sufferings, becoming like him in his death, and so, somehow, attaining to the resurrection from the dead" (Philippians 3:10–11). In our desire to know Christ, it is easy to say yes to the "power of his resurrection," where God is doing great and mighty things in our lives. That sounds fantastic, but it represents only half of what it means to know Christ. The other element of truly embracing and knowing Christ is the "participation in his sufferings." It is at that point we hear the voice of our Savior, "You do not want to leave too, do you?" (John 6:67).

Following Jesus is not easy as it requires us to let go of our lives and embrace both the "power of his resurrection" and the "participation in his sufferings." Where does this suffering come from? It will come as we live out God's purpose for our lives in this world (Ephesians 2:10) and primarily through the hands and lives of people who have not experienced the grace and salvation of Christ, who are still controlled by the ways of this broken and fallen world. (Satan, of course, plays an enormous role in the opposition and suffering that comes our way—Ephesians 6:12—see Day 13).

The more intimate and meaningful these relationships are to our lives, the deeper the pain, grief, and loneliness we will bear when serving Christ (and those He puts in our path) starts to conflict with the demands of those closest to us. When we face hostility and rejection from our inner circle, will we allow our love for Jesus to be torn and divided as we try to find a workable and "peaceful" compromise with our adversaries, or will we be willing to embrace "his sufferings" so we can share in His glory, comfort, joy, and grace (1 Peter 4:12–19)? Experiencing the fullness of Christ's love for us and God's provision in our lives requires us to face and embrace the suffering that comes our way because we belong to Him.

Suffering is not pleasant, but it will always be part of our walk and fellowship with Jesus because Jesus demands absolute loyalty to Him over all other relationships and priorities (Matthew 10:34–39). The deeper we go with Him, the more we love and know Him, the more we will experience hurts from those opposed to Him and His work in this world. We must persevere through our sufferings to mature in our Christian faith (James 1:2–4). When things are at their toughest, it is good to remind ourselves of what Jesus endured on our behalf:

> . . . and let us run with perseverance the race marked out for us, fixing our eyes on Jesus, the pioneer and perfecter of our faith. For the joy set before him he endured the cross, scorning its shame, and sat down at the right hand of the throne of God. Consider him who endured such opposition from sinners, so that you will not grow weary and lose heart. (Hebrews 12:1b–3)

Continue to pray for them, keep your heart open to them, proclaim the gospel to them when given an open door and receptive heart, but continue walking in the direction your Lord is headed. Let the fear of people and the desire to be acceptable to them dissipate into the beautiful and loving eyes of your Savior.

Father, give me an undivided heart today to serve You. Show me the things in my life that are competing for my loyalty: _____. I lay each of them before Your feet. Show me how to align my life to Your will this very day so that my first love will be for You and Your work in this world above everyone and everything else. Amen!

Meditation: I want to know Christ—yes, and the power of his resurrection and participation in his sufferings, becoming like him in his death, and so, somehow, attaining to the resurrection from the dead. (Philippians 3:10–11)

Worship: "Give Me Jesus" (Fernando Ortega)

Tips: Betrayal by a close friend is one of the deepest hurts! To help with the healing process, write a letter to that person but do not send the letter. Keep it concise and capture what they did to you to break the trust between you and them. Emotions may run high at this point but try minimizing their influence in your letter. You want to capture what motivated them to do what they did to you. Remember Judas betrayed Jesus for wealth! A mere thirty silver coins!

Nevertheless, some of the people went out on the seventh day to gather it [manna], but they found none.

Exodus 16:27

DAY 20

HARVEST TIME IN CHAMPAGNE

The Dry Bones of Not Stopping!

What is the busiest season of the year in Champagne? That would be harvest time, when over 100,000 pickers descend upon Champagne for three weeks of picking grapes. It sounds like a romantic, joyful experience to be among the vineyards, harvesting grapes, drinking Champagne, and enjoying French bread and cheese. In fact, it is if you enjoy the outdoors, gardening, hard work, and working alongside others with a shared passion for vineyards, wine, and French cuisine. People take time off work to participate in the harvest. Now if you are thinking this might be an experience for you, you need to be flexible with your schedule as the actual harvest dates fluctuate year after year, depending on the warmth of the growing season. Harvest can start as early as August or as late as October. However, once the date is set you better be ready to work and work hard. There is no rest for those who are

Father, my heart is anxious about my labor and toils. Reprioritize my Sabbath day so it will be focused on You and the renewal You promise to give me and others who set aside this day and cease from our labors. Show me the things I have allowed to bind me mentally, physically, spiritually, and emotionally and set me free. Show me the new habits I am to form for this coming Sabbath. Amen.

Meditation: However, some of them paid no attention to Moses: they kept part of it until morning, but it was full of maggots and began to smell. So Moses was angry with them. (Exodus 16:20)

Worship: "Indescribable" (Chris Tomlin)

Tips: The goal is to recognize the things that bind your life and instead put into practice the things God gives us to free us and refresh our lives on the Sabbath. Ways to get started: (1) Be intentional about the Sabbath. Preplan the day instead of allowing the day to unfold randomly. (2) Celebrate God. (3) Avoid technology, especially the internet and the television. Instead, enjoy God's good creation. If you still want to watch a movie, choose a show about nature. (4) Do not focus on getting things accomplished. (5) Look to renew or refresh others who need to be freed from their own toils, sorrows, and pains of this life.

Pride goes before destruction,
a haughty spirit before a fall.

Proverbs 16:18

DAY 21

UNPREDICTABLE WEATHER

The Dry Bones of Pride

Champagne is either vintage or non-vintage. Vintage Champagne is made with the grapes of a single year's harvest and will be labeled with the year of the harvest. Non-vintage Champagne is made with a blend of wine from grape harvests over several years to produce a house Champagne that is consistent year after year (the majority of bottles sold are of the non-vintage variety). As you probably guessed, vintage Champagne is made from the best of the grapes from the best of the vineyards. What you may not have known is that vintage Champagne is not made every year. A vintage Champagne is only made when the grapes are of exceptional or above average quality for that year—otherwise all the Champagne made that year will be in the non-vintage category. Furthermore, the quality of grapes for any particular year is determined primarily by one thing, the weather. It would be pretty foolish for any Champagne house to declare in May that they will be producing a vintage Champagne for that year. It is better to humbly wait to see what God sends your way and be thankful for the harvest, whether vintage or not.

Unfortunately, too many of us are very prone to making declarations in May without regard to the unpredictability and haphazardness of life as it truly unfolds. What I mean is that we can allow pride to sneak into our lives and blind us to reality. Pride is easy to see in others but is difficult to discern in ourselves. Unfortunately, if we are not careful, we may end up lying in a bed of dry bones from Ezekiel's vision, for the Bible says "Pride goes before destruction, a haughty spirit before a fall" (Proverbs 16:18), and again, "God opposes the proud" (James 4:6).

Pride blinds us, hardens our hearts, deafens our ears, and separates us from God, people, and His created order. In contrast, humility is submissive in its commitment to God (His will, words, and ways) and to meeting the deep and current needs of others. Pride is stubborn, compromises the Word of God, and hates people; however, humility gives us insight, refreshes our soul, and brings us closer to God, His world, and people. Humility fully knows the inheritance God has in store (Matthew 5:3) is much better than the temporary pleasures pride deceptively dangles before our eyes—pleasures that will either vanish or leave a lasting stench as soon as we reach for them. Humility does not hide behind a false front of perfection or things being under control. Humility is vulnerable to being rejected and admitting failure. Humility is counter to the pride of life (1 John 2:16) and will always result in peace.

Humility is what drives serving others for the sole purpose of serving them regardless of how they treat us. Our goal should be to serve them as best we can in the Lord's eyes, not their eyes. We will often serve ungrateful and mean-spirited individuals who will never be satisfied with our work. If we bear up under it and do what is right in the

Lord's eyes, we will be rewarded by Him (Ephesians 6:5–8). Though it may be difficult, we have been given the perfect model, the one who died for our sins (Philippians 2:3–11). The proud will only inherit distress, we will reap joy. After all, our Savior is "gentle and humble in heart" and when we humble ourselves before Him, we "will find rest for" our "souls" (Matthew 11:29).

Lord, give me a humble heart today, ears that are quick to listen, emotions that are slow to rise, and a mouth that is slow to speak. Holy Spirit, produce in me today the fruit of meekness (gentleness) so I may exhibit my Savior's life to those I meet today. Help me discern when pride comes knocking on the door and keep me from making any decisions that are not based on Your will, whether through Your Word or through someone You send to me. I rely on You to defend me and help me give a fair hearing to all those I meet today. Help me stay quiet and listen and wait for Your voice today. Help me not to rush. Amen.

Meditation: God opposes the proud but shows favor to the humble. (James 4:6)

Worship: "I Surrender" (Hillsong)

Tips: No matter how much we think we know about a certain topic or a situation, our knowledge does not compare to God's knowledge. His knowledge is perfect and He knows the plans He will bring into existence and how the future will unfold. It's best to put aside your "expertise" and be ready to listen and understand from God's perspective. It will save you from the unnecessary heartache of going down the wrong road and will open an unexpected opportunity to bring Him glory.

But you are a chosen people, a royal priesthood, a holy nation, God's special possession, that you may declare the praises of him who called you out of darkness into his wonderful light.

1 Peter 2:9

RESERVED FOR THE CHAMPAGNE HOUSE

The Dry Bones of Indistinctness

A s the trucks roll out of every Champagne house, delivering the latest product to the public, some of the bottles are left in the cellar, reserved for the exclusive use of the Champagne house. The purpose for which these bottles are kept varies. Some of the inventory is dedicated to customer tastings during tours of the Champagne house. Other bottles are utilized by the Chef de Cave and his/her team to monitor the quality of the champagne as it ages. Still other bottles may be kept hidden away to be opened at key anniversary milestones of the Champagne house. Some houses even store a few bottles away in the cellar for legacy purposes, potentially never to be opened. (Möet & Chandon has bottles from the late nineteenth century kept in its cellars.) When you think of these bottles, reserved by the house, you know the house takes special pride as each bottle represents the tradition, the heritage, and the glory of that house. They are distinct. In essence, you could say these bottles are holy, set apart for the exclusive purposes of the Champagne house only.

While it may be a stretch to use the word *holiness* to describe a bottle of Champagne—though the 1928 Krug may be the closest to deserving the distinction—it is one of the essential qualities of being a follower of Jesus. Holiness carries a dual meaning. First, it describes someone who has been reserved or set aside by God for His purpose and His pleasure. The second aspect of holiness is to be morally pure. It is to live a life of distinctiveness, unambiguousness, and moral fortitude, "but you are a chosen people, a royal priesthood, a holy nation, God's special possession, that you may declare the praises of him who called you out of darkness into his wonderful light" (1 Peter 2:9).

It is also a command of God, "I am the LORD your God; consecrate yourselves and be holy, because I am holy" (Leviticus 11:44). And because God is holy, our spirits should yearn for and delight in holiness. Despite all this goodness before us, there is one thing that can draw our hearts away from the beauty of holiness and pull us into the dark recesses of Ezekiel's valley of dry bones—our sinful nature or as the Bible also calls it, our flesh.

It is our sinful nature (our flesh) that is most susceptible to compromise. "Those who live according to the flesh have their minds set on what the flesh desires; but those who live in accordance with the Spirit have their minds set on what the Spirit desires. The mind governed by the flesh is death, but the mind governed by the Spirit is life and peace" (Romans 8:5–6). When we choose the shadows instead of the path of obedience, our way will be dark and hazy, filled with confusion and fear. We will continue dwelling in these shadows until we fully give up the lie we can both live as the culture around us lives and also be set aside by God for His exclusive use.

Perhaps this vision God gave His prophet Jeremiah concerning Israel will help us clearly see our issue from God's vantage point:

> After Jeconiah son of Jehoiakim king of Judah and the officials, the skilled workers and the artisans of Judah were carried into exile from Jerusalem to Babylon by Nebuchadnezzar king of Babylon, the LORD showed me two baskets of figs placed in front of the temple of the LORD. One basket had very good figs, like those that ripen early; the other basket had very bad figs, so bad they could not be eaten.
>
> Then the LORD asked me, "What do you see, Jeremiah?"
>
> "Figs," I answered. "The good ones are very good, but the bad ones are so bad they cannot be eaten."
>
> Then the word of the LORD came to me: "This is what the LORD, the God of Israel, says: 'Like these good figs, I regard as good the exiles from Judah, whom I sent away from this place to the land of the Babylonians. My eyes will watch over them for their good, and I will bring them back to this land. I will build them up and not tear them down; I will plant them and not uproot them. I will give them a heart to know me, that I am the LORD. They will be my people, and I will be their God, for they will return to me with all their heart.
>
> "'But like the bad figs, which are so bad they cannot be eaten,' says the LORD, 'so will I deal with

Zedekiah king of Judah, his officials and the sur-
vivors from Jerusalem, whether they remain in this
land or live in Egypt. I will make them abhorrent
and an offense to all the kingdoms of the earth, a
reproach and a byword, a curse and an object of
ridicule, wherever I banish them. I will send the
sword, famine and plague against them until they
are destroyed from the land I gave to them and
their ancestors.'" (Jeremiah 24:1–10)

We all have been given two baskets from which to take
fruit that will impact how we live our lives on this earth and
determine the final outcome of our lives. Only one basket
results in a life of distinctiveness.

---

*Father, reveal to me every area of my life that has not
been set aside exclusively for Your use and pleasure.
Where I have my hands in both baskets of figs, forgive
me for choosing the following inedible figs _____.
Help me change my ways and give me the courage to
let go of these "rotten figs" I have deemed "good" in my
life. I choose Your holiness in my thoughts, actions and
words for this day and each day You have ordained for
me until You take me home (Psalm 90:12). Amen.*

Meditation: But you are a chosen people, a royal priesthood, a holy nation, God's special possession, that you may declare the praises of him who called you out of darkness into his wonderful light. (1 Peter 2:9)

Worship: "Just as I Am" (Charlotte Elliott)

Tips: Go for a long walk with God and discuss the areas in your life that are distinct and those that are not distinct. Build upon the areas that are distinct and seek direction on what needs to be done to make the indistinct, distinct. As you proceed, expect your spirit to be strengthened and your mind to be focused as a healthy spiritual vigor begins to permeate your life.

"Blessed are the merciful, for they will be shown mercy."

Matthew 5:7

DAY 23

A CHAMPAGNE CRITIC

The Dry Bones of Condemning the Innocent

It would seem that few jobs in the world would be more desired than to be a sparkling wine critic. Everything about it sounds like a cushy assignment. You sample the best sparkling wines in the world, travel to some of the most interesting and beautiful places on this planet and enjoy the unique and rich cuisine heritage of each place you visit. The icing on the cake is of course the tasting and rating of the sparkling wines coming from the Champagne region, the pinnacle of your job description. Of course, when you finish the tasting of the Champagnes, you will need to write up a review of each producer you rate and assign it a score between 0 and 100, but that is also what makes the job so enjoyable and yet potentially disheartening as well. You see, your reviews are not just read by consumers and wine merchants, but by those impacted the most by your rating, the

Champagne producers. The issue really arises when the current year's growing season is negatively impacted by the one factor outside everyone's control, the weather. In times such as these, it is best to wrap your entire review within the blanket of the difficult growing season. After all, there is no reason to use your position of power to condemn and destroy the reputations of these fine Champagne houses who are trying their best to make the most of a very challenging situation.

Alas, one of the most heart-sinking events in life is experiencing the merciless actions of others directed toward innocent people, especially when it impacts us or someone we know well. It becomes more unbearable when their actions affect a major area of our lives such as our families or places of employment. These are the people who condemn the innocent. They rob people of their sense of security and worth, creating an atmosphere where lives can be instantaneously uprooted in a negative way. How we respond when faced with such people determines whether we continue on the pleasant highways of our Lord or take the wide exit ramps to Ezekiel's valley of dry bones filled with distress.

Only an unnatural response to their actions will help us navigate this segment of the highway. It is the passing lane of forgiveness. Forgiveness keeps us on the delightful highway of our Lord and avoids the anxiety that will consume our hearts. Let God deal with them and respond with compassion when mistreated and wronged.

Look, the path of mercy is the path of God. Merciful people seek to restore that which is broken. Mercy renews that which has been wronged. Mercy delights in showing eager hands of compassion to those who are hurting in life and is willing to bear the cost of forgiveness shown toward someone who has hurt us deeply. Jesus taught "Blessed are the merciful, for they will be shown mercy" (Matthew 5:7), or in the words of James, "Speak and act as those who are going to be judged by the law that gives freedom, because judgment without mercy will be shown to anyone who has not been merciful. Mercy triumphs over judgment" (James 2:12–13). Those who show mercy have the heart of God as His light shines brightest amid our hurts, when we extend mercy to others, and forgiveness to those who have wronged us. For we show mercy for His sake because we have experienced His hands of mercy extended to us.

Lord, today I choose the fresh air and wide-open fields of mercy that are before me. Today I forgive the following people who have harmed me: _____.
For those I have harmed, help me ask for their forgiveness and show me how to make the situation right in Your eyes. Finally, Lord bring into my life those I need to extend a hand of mercy toward. Amen.

Meditation: Be merciful to me, LORD, for I am in distress; my eyes grow weak with sorrow, my soul and body with grief. (Psalm 31:9)

"Blessed are the merciful, for they will be shown mercy. . . . Blessed are the peacemakers, for they will be called children of God." (Matthew 5:7, 9)

Worship: "Amazing Grace" (John Newton)

Tips: To truly forgive someone is to give up our claim to have the situation made right. It is hard to do for it goes against our desire for justice. However, it is the only course we can take to gain back our freedom from the one who ill-treated us, otherwise we will always be looking to that person to rectify the situation and that may never happen. Do not allow unforgiveness to rule your heart; it is a merciless guest that will steal your joy and peace.

Be kind and compassionate to one another, forgiving each other,
just as in Christ God forgave you.

Ephesians 4:32

GENTLE WITH THE CHAMPAGNE GRAPES

The Dry Bones of Unkindness

Did you know that all grapes in Champagne are hand-picked? The reason for this is quite simple. One of the main grapes used in Champagne is Pinot Noir, which has a dark skin. The pulp is clear, but the skin is dark and so the harvesters must be careful not to crush the grape and allow the skins to taint the clear juice. Now if the Champagne house is going for a Rosé, then its fine, but if they are aiming for a golden hue, then they need to be careful. It does not take that many dark grape skins bleeding into the clear liquid to change the color of the whole batch. So, it would be wise for the harvesters to be kind and gentle with the grape harvest, because once a batch is tainted you cannot undo the damage.

Obviously, no one harvesting grapes in Champagne is going to be so careless as to manhandle or deliberately damage the grapes. If one so dared, other employees would see with horror and the offender would be quickly rushed out of the vineyard, banned for life. No one would be so negligent and yet when it comes to people, we can all quickly remember a time when someone was either deliberately or thoughtlessly unkind to us. Worse, we may remember a time when we were the one who was dishing out the unkindness. Unkindness stains everything it touches. It is harsh, bitter, inconsiderate, and unloving of the needs and desires of others.

Unkindness treats others with coldness and neglect. It deflates and crushes the heart. It steals life and joy from us. It demotivates and distracts us from using our talents and gifts to serve and love the Lord. Unfortunately, unkindness is also one of the leading reasons we will find ourselves in the midst of the dry bones of Ezekiel's valley. Either through our own unkind deeds and words or by allowing the unkindness of others to shape our lives negatively, we find ourselves in this valley of cold and unfeeling dry bones struggling to get out. The impact on our faith is almost immediate as the sense of our Lord's joy and love seems distant.

Of course, we should never be unkind—and when it happens, we should be quick to apologize with sincerity and humility. However, the greatest risk to our spiritual lives is the unkind deeds and words of others who do not apologize nor show remorse. And the closer these folks are to our lives, the greater the negative impact they can have on us. If we are not careful to guard our hearts, we will inadvertently give these folks the power to lock us up in a spiritual and emotional dungeon of our making, waiting for justice and restoration that will never come to visit us.

The hardest step out of the valley of dry bones is to let go of our false expectations and unrealistic need that others should be kind to us. For reasons only known to God, some people are just unkind and unapologetic for their behavior.

They have chosen to live among the dry bones of Ezekiel's valley. We do not need to live with them. Avoid their traps. Walk or run away and never look back. As followers of Jesus, we will encounter the worst of the unkind, the greatest of the unjust, and the epitome of mean-spirited people. Do not lose heart but remember who you belong to, for He has allowed these individuals to come into your life to test you and strengthen your faith in Him. Set your heart on seeking God, walk away from your dungeon cell, and ask Him for His perspective.

You see you were made for kindness, first shown to us by our heavenly father (Titus 3:3–8) and then to be modeled by us toward others (Ephesians 4:32). Kindness is warm heartedness and tenderness toward every person we meet and interact with today. It refreshes and brightens the soul and brings joy to life. Like a warm blanket and cup of hot chocolate on a cold night, kindness soothes and comforts us through the difficulties, struggles, and toils of life. Kindness gives strength to the broken-hearted and the discouraged and welcomes them with healing arms and a warm smile. It is magnanimous, hospitable, and friendly. Kindness draws people in removing fear and softening people to receive God's love. Should not our lives be filled to overflowing with one act of kindness followed by another? It is our privilege and duty to inspire and elevate all those around us by demonstrating the kindness we have personally received from our heavenly Father, through Christ.

_____

*Father, forgive me for being unkind to _____
and show me how to make it right. Forgive me for
holding on to anger and bitterness because of an unkind*

word or deed by _____ toward me. Thank You for Your ongoing kindness toward me and show me who I can be extraordinarily kind (Acts 28:1–2) toward today. Amen!

Meditation: Be kind and compassionate to one another, forgiving each other, just as in Christ God forgave you. (Ephesians 4:32)

Worship: "Lifesong" (Casting Crowns)

Tips: Identify someone you know who does not deserve to be shown any kindness. My guess is that name came to mind quickly. Plan something to show that person kindness. Also, identify someone who is struggling in life. Take the time to do something that shows them kindness. Pray through each act of kindness so your act fits that person's need. God will show you what to do. He knows what will soften the hardest of hearts and renew the spirit of the one who is crushed. Do not set any expectations on how someone will respond. The Lord will reward you by confirming your action through the joy you experience in your heart. This is the joy that originates and radiates from your heavenly Father who is well pleased with His child.

Also, see previous Tip on Forgiveness on page 136.

A cheerful heart is good medicine, but a crushed spirit dries up the bones.

Proverbs 17:22

BITTER CHAMPAGNE!

The Dry Bones of a Crushed Spirit

The process for making a sparkling bottle of Champagne begins with the crushing of the grapes. The traditional Champagne grape varietals—Chardonnay, Pinot Meunier and Pinot Noir—are hand harvested and carefully placed into large Champagne presses that begin the work to extract the coveted juice from these grand grapes. The freshly squeezed liquid is then transferred to fermentation tanks where yeast is added, and within a few months and a few more production steps you have a bottle of Champagne ready to pop open. One word of caution though, the crushing of the grapes needs to be done precisely, otherwise you could press too hard and end up extracting some of the bitter flavors from the grape seeds that will leave your Champagne with a sour aftertaste. That does not make for a joyful celebration.

Now don't worry. Getting a bottle of bitter Champagne is highly unlikely, if not close to impossible, but if it were to happen, rest assured that the wine shop will eagerly take back the bottle and give you a new one. However, what you don't do is continue to drink it or lament that you have a bottle of bitter Champagne. That would be silly. Spit it out, hop in the car, and go get a new bottle.

Seems simple! If only life were as easy to navigate as returning a bitter bottle of Champagne when faced with life's hardships, worries, great disappointments, severe trials, or deepest sorrows that come to roost in our lives and linger for months, years, or lifetimes. Without warning we can find ourselves facing Ezekiel's valley of dry bones, a bitter place, without hope and full of despair. If we allow these things to take root in our hearts, they will crush our spirits, much like over-pressing grapes will release the bitter flavors from their seeds.

Perhaps you find yourself fighting hard to stay out of Ezekiel's valley of hopelessness and growing tired of the fight. Perhaps you have already lost the fight and your zest for life is just one of those "bones that were very dry." Maybe your crushed spirit is the result of allowing yourself to become consumed with the fight that is out of your control rather than consumed with Jesus who will fill your heart with joy as He leads you through your "valley of the shadow of death." He is the One who provides when the money has dried up. He is the One who redeems when you think you have missed out on God's best for your life. He is the One who forgives when your past has left you with deep regrets. He is the One who heals when sickness, death, sorrow, or a troubled heart comes knocking on your door. And He is the One who loves when the circumstances of your life cause you to wonder whether your life has any worth.

When holding the seed of a crushed spirit, we can either choose to nurture it as it grows and destroys our lives or we can toss it out and choose God's offer of peace of mind that leads to our ultimate joy. "Do not be anxious about anything, but in every situation, by prayer and petition, with thanksgiving, present your requests to God. And the peace of God, which transcends all understanding, will guard your hearts and your minds in Christ Jesus" (Philippians 4:6–7). Each day we are invited to turn our attention to Jesus and our eyes away from everything else and in return He gives us His peace, His rest, and His inexpressible joy (Luke 2:10–11; John 15:11; Matthew 11:28–30).

As the psalmist reminds us, "weeping may stay for the night, but rejoicing comes in the morning" (Psalm 30:5). So why are you still holding on to that seed of a crushed spirit? Throw it over your shoulder and venture forth toward Jesus and surrender your life and this day to the One who was "crushed for our iniquities" (Isaiah 53:5).

I look to You, my Good Shepherd, and surrender to You the thing causing my spirit to feel crushed and defeated. I acknowledge I am not able to bring resolution to the current situation, but I declare over this deep hurt that Your peace and joy would overflow in abundance and Your love would wash away the bitter situation and leave behind wholeness and grace. You are my Shepherd and You told me Your sheep hear Your voice. Speak grace and mercy into my life Lord so my heart may rejoice and give thanks and feast once again on your perfect Word and drink deeply of your effervescent love for me (Isaiah 55:1–2). Amen.

Meditation: A cheerful heart is good medicine, but a crushed spirit dries up the bones (Proverbs 17:22).

Worship: "Even If" (MercyMe)

Tips: It's okay to cry! There are situations beyond our ability to grasp and process with our minds. Sometimes weeping before the Lord is the only thing that can bring healing to our broken hearts. Tears shed in the midst of our shattered dreams have the capacity to wash away the bitterness. Grieve with a close friend if you are able. Whatever you do, do not allow your emotions to bottle up and destroy you. Weep and let your deep sorrow pour out to your Lord.

"Seek first his kingdom and his righteousness, and all these things will be given to you as well."

Matthew 6:33

DAY 26

OUT OF CHAMPAGNE

The Dry Bones of Fearing an Empty Bank Account

The days leading up to New Year's Eve are some of the busiest times at the local wine, beer, and spirits shop. The shop merchant and her employees are busy helping customers, answering questions about food and wine pairings, going back and forth between the stock room and the retail floor to replenish empty wine racks and refrigerators as customers clear out the merchant's wonderful selection of drinks. It is a festive time at these stores. Of course, the main beverage on everyone's mind are the bottles of Champagne that will be uncorked at midnight to bring in the New Year. Now the merchant is going to stock enough Champagne to meet everyone's needs, but it is up to you to purchase enough to meet the needs of your party guests. After all, it would be embarrassing to run out of Champagne before everyone has had a sip when the clock strikes midnight.

Running out of Champagne might be embarrassing, but running short of money can be a major cause of worry and depression. Perhaps times have been tight for you and the anxiety level is high in the house. Your marriage is stressed, and the expenses seem to grow faster than the income. You remember in times past it was not always this way, but times are different now. Maybe you are hand-to-mouth or maybe a job loss has set you back or your current job just doesn't meet your living expenses. You have tried to find new employment with a livable salary, but it seems every door is closed to you. You go left and the way is blocked. You go right and there is a detour. You are at a loss as to what to do because nothing seems to work. You are stuck. You have become one of those "bones that were very dry" (Ezekiel 37:2) in Ezekiel's vision. Perhaps God is using this desperate and impossible situation in your finances to teach you and those closest to you a valuable lesson on who is really in charge of caring for your life.

Your ability to provide for your needs and your family's needs is not dependent on your skills, your titles, your degrees, your hustle, your personality, your current employer, your current job status, or who you know. None of these things matter! Do not put your trust in these things, ever! God already knows you need food, clothing and housing—the practical things of life. Jesus told us not to worry about these things nor be anxious, for our Father would provide for us as He does the birds each day (Matthew 6:24–34). What matters is whether you have faith in God as your provider or not. Will you stop your worry and let your anxious thoughts be stilled and look intently at your Father and let Him care for your needs?

Now your heavenly Father might use the normal things of life to provide for your needs (the things listed above) or do something completely new and unexpected in your life. Either way it still requires you to stop with the panicking and begin to listen to your Father's voice. He said He will provide for His children, and He means it. God will breathe life into the dry bones of your finances, but you must trust

Him completely by stopping and hearing His voice. What is He saying to you right now?

Look, you are not the only one He has done this for, nor will you be the last. When God brought His people "out of Egypt, out of the land of slavery" and led them "through the vast and dreadful wilderness, that thirsty and waterless land, with its venomous snakes and scorpions," (Deuteronomy 8:14–15) on the way to the Promised Land, He initiated a teaching experience for them as well. Moses describes it this way: "He humbled you, causing you to hunger and then feeding you with manna, which neither you nor your ancestors had known, to teach you that man does not live on bread alone but on every word that comes from the mouth of the LORD" (Deuteronomy 8:3) and to "test you so that in the end it might go well with you" (Deuteronomy 8:16).

The Israelites were to live a life of dependency on and expectancy for God as their sole provider and it is the same for us today as well! We just need to recognize that fact and adjust our lives accordingly. He is the one who signs our checks! He is our boss who hires us out to others! He is our Father who cares deeply for us and our families! And He is the one who owns everything in the world and can choose to give you and your family anything He wants. His wallet never runs dry but overflows with abundance! He is sufficient to provide for all our needs (2 Corinthians 9:8–11)!

Now the wilderness doesn't sound like a great place to be. It is not supposed to be pleasant, but it is how God disciplines and trains His sons and daughters whom He loves deeply (Deuteronomy 8:5) to show them how life is to be lived. It is a "dreadful" and "waterless" place filled with "venomous snakes and scorpions" and it is also the only path we are given to experience the supernatural provision of God, to avoid growing prideful in our riches (Deuteronomy 8:14), to remember to thank Him and praise Him for His provision

(Deuteronomy 8:10) and to never forget Him. "Remember the Lord your God, for it is he who gives you the ability to produce wealth, and so confirms his covenant, which he swore to your ancestors, as it is today" (Deuteronomy 8:18).

Living a life of dependency and expectancy is a life that has surrendered itself completely to the promises of our Lord, knowing those promises include His provision to us. When He tells us to "seek first his kingdom and his righteous, and all these things [food, clothes, housing] will be given to you as well" (Matthew 6:33), Jesus is telling us how to order our lives properly within our Father's world. What is most important is serving Him in the work He gives us to do. This means we are to serve our customers, our bosses, our staff, our families, and anyone else the Lord brings into our lives as if we are serving Jesus Himself. It is through working and serving in the specific location He assigns to us and the people we come in contact with that He gives our daily bread—food, clothing and housing—and cares for us (Matthew 6:11, 31–34).

So set aside your financial worries and anxieties, hear your Father's voice, and let Him show you the work He wants you to do. Watch as your Father transforms your finances to meet your daily needs (Isaiah 61:6–7; Joel 2:24–26; Proverbs 10:22). And who knows, perhaps God will use you as His financial agent to help someone else struggling to make ends meet.

Lord, breathe life into my finances by Your Holy Spirit. Cause me and my family to prosper once again. Thank You. Forgive me for holding on to a stingy heart. Open my eyes wide to see the people and places You want me to serve. Help me trust You daily for my needs, knowing that all my tomorrows are also in Your hands. Show me how to be generous with those in need with the resources You have provided to me and give me a willing and joyful heart to do so. Grant me success in the place where You put me so I may faithfully bear witness to Jesus to everyone You send me to serve. Amen.

Meditation: "Seek first his kingdom and his righteousness, and all these things will be given to you as well." (Matthew 6:33)

Worship: "Call on Jesus" (Nicole C. Mullen)

Tips: Tithing opens God's warehouse of blessing and is the only place God says to test Him on a matter of obedience and faith with a promise to provide for our financial support and provision (Malachi 3:10):

> "Bring the whole tithe into the storehouse, that there may be food in my house. Test me in this," says the LORD Almighty, "and see if I will not throw open the floodgates of heaven and pour out so much blessing that there will not be room enough to store it."

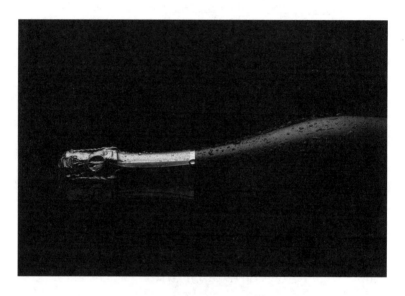

For you know that it was not with perishable things such as silver or gold that you were redeemed from the empty way of life handed down to you from your ancestors, but with the precious blood of Christ, a lamb without blemish or defect.

1 Peter 1:18–19

EXTRAVAGANT CHAMPAGNE

The Dry Bones of Fearing Missing God's Best

The 2002 Krug Brut Blanc de Noirs Champagne Clos d'Ambonnay, rated 99 out of 100 by Wine Spectator, retails for an astronomical $2,500 a bottle (750ml).[4] That's a whopping $400 a glass for almost pure perfection. Now, I do not know about you, but most people could not afford such an expensive bottle of bubbly, nor if they could afford it, would they actually buy it. It seems like this bottle is reserved for the collectors and the folks with wealth beyond measure, definitely out of reach for the rest of us. What a shame. It would have been such a treat to taste such an extraordinary and extravagant bottle of Champagne.

While the best of Champagne may be reserved for a few fortunate souls, that is not the situation when it comes to experiencing God's best for our lives. Not only has God made it possible to experience His best, but He is also actively wooing each of us every moment of our lives to say yes to His best. Yet how many of us are now facing painful and unexpected circumstances that are shrouding God's best and filling our minds with anxious, troubled thoughts? Perhaps our own sense of worthiness, or our self-imposed limits regarding what God is willing to do for us, have artificially lowered our expectations of His best. Some of us are perhaps wrestling with past sins and missed opportunities and the idea of God's best is something He reserves for other people. Whatever the reason, we are now wondering whether God's best has stampeded by us in the early hours while we slept with only a dust cloud remaining. And as the dust settles to the ground, the hope of green pastures and quiet waters is dashed as the silhouettes of dry and dusty bones emerge. We are now staring blank-faced into Ezekiel's valley of dashed dreams, far from God's best, wondering what has happened and scraping whatever leftovers we can find to make it through life.

Unfortunately, our circumstances, personal expectations, and past mistakes can refract our vision of who God is and what He is doing in our lives. We mistakenly conclude that the best years are in the past. Actually, His best is rooted in His fatherly love for each of us, displayed in the most extravagant way through the shed blood of Christ on the cross to redeem each of us from our bondage to sin. The apostle Peter puts it this way: "For you know that it was not with perishable things such as silver or gold that you were redeemed from the empty way of life handed down to you from your ancestors, but with the precious blood of Christ, a lamb without blemish or defect" (1 Peter 1:18–19). Our redemption through the precious blood of Christ means we are wanted by God. If we are wanted by God, why should we ever doubt He also wants His very best for our lives?

God's best is neither earned nor a prize to be won! It is not an elusive shadow that appears for a moment and then vanishes if we are not alert enough to grasp it. Instead, God invites each of us to experience His best in our lives through one of the most generous invitations we will ever hear:

> "Come, all you who are thirsty, come to the waters; and you who have no money, come, buy and eat! Come, buy wine and milk without money and without cost. Why spend money on what is not bread, and your labor on what does not satisfy? Listen, listen to me, and eat what is good, and you will delight in the richest of fare." (Isaiah 55:1–2)

Does that sound like a stingy God to you?

There is a catch, however, two of them in fact. It is the fine print that goes along with God's best. Fortunately, as is the case with Champagne, the fine print provides us with essential information and warnings prior to opening the bottle of God's best. First, our Father might point out things in our lives that are not according to His will. Do not despair! This is part of the process of receiving God's best. Get rid of whatever He identifies, whether it be a sin or something good that God is replacing with something better. Sin or second-rate good is not God's best for us. Second, His best will always be in an unexpected form though consistent with our calling, gifts, and sensibilities. It is at this point we will face a faith decision. Do we trust Him or not?

You see our Father has rooms filled with "Krug's Clos d'Ambonnay." Bottles beyond measure sitting upon tables clothed with the finest and most expensive of linen fabrics. Hand-blown crystal flutes overflowing with golden bubbles. Succulent fare, every item perfectly paired with the featured

Champagne as if both were made to be together and never apart. It is a feast, a sight, and excites all our senses. Gratitude and joy bubbling up in our hearts and overflowing with praise and love for our Lord, as we realize how much He truly loves and wants the best for us. All of this is ours when we say yes to His best.

So let us come to our loving Father with all our hearts and set aside our fears that we will miss His best. Our Father's desire is for us to drink deeply from His extravagant and extraordinary love each day of our lives. It is the best way to live!

Lord, I want Your very best. Show me anything in my life not in line with Your very best for my life. Forgive me for the following sins _____. Help me surrender even the good things in my life _____ You have brought to my mind. Show me what is best for my life and give me the courage to say yes to Your perfect will. Amen!

Meditation: His blood cleanses us so we can serve God with a clear conscious. (Hebrews 9:14)

He who did not spare his own Son, but gave him up for us all—how will he not also, along with him, graciously give us all things? (Romans 8:32)

Worship: "Be Still, My Soul" (Katharina A. von Schlegel) or "Be Still" (Hillsong)

Tips: Sometimes our own rebellion has caused God's best to be delayed in our lives. Search your heart to see if there is any sin and confess it. If you have neglected an assignment He has given you, finish it. God's best will arrive with speed once your relationship is right with Him.

"Come now, let us settle the matter," says the LORD, *"Though your sins are like scarlet, they shall be as white as snow; though they are red as crimson, they shall be like wool."*

Isaiah 1:18

DAY 28

A CLEAN CHAMPAGNE GLASS

The Dry Bones of Fearing God's Rejection

Have you ever hoisted a Champagne glass above eye level? Allowed the light of the room to penetrate the glass? Gazed upon the Champagne now engulfed in light? And watched the bubbles float to the top, sparkling in all their glory? It is a sight to behold, an unexpected beauty, too amazing to capture in words. However, holding up the glass to the light also reveals something else, the cleanliness of the glass. Without a clean glass the Champagne does not sparkle, in fact, the focus is no longer on the Champagne but on the dirtiness of the glass. The solution? Throw away the glass and get a new one? No! No one would do that. That would be a total waste of a perfectly good and valuable glass. Instead, clean the glass both on the outside and on the inside with washing soda and water until it sparkles and then pour in the Champagne and enjoy. A simple solution for a simple problem: wash, rinse, and pour.

In truth, we are not very different than that glass—we are not entirely clean, especially when God's light is shining on us, through the conviction of the Holy Spirit and the Word of God. If the light were simply a comparison between us and other people, then we might be able to live with whatever imperfections we notice. However, the light is shining so brightly that our initial response is to hide. This was Adam's and Eve's response when they sinned by eating the fruit they were warned to avoid. It is a natural response because we are ashamed and feel disgraced. We hide because we are driven by a deep-seated fear that perhaps we will ultimately be rejected by God.

The thunderous voice in our head that says "Hide! Bury it!" is none other than the tyrannical voice of sin as it lies to us. Yet when we respond to this voice by then covering our shame and disgrace, we start to hear the sound of rattling bones in Ezekiel's valley. On the bones are written the words *overwhelming, dreadful, consequences,* and we shudder in fear. In our attempt to cover up our actions and motives we have actually chosen a fruitless and barren wasteland away from our Father's love. Why do we find ourselves here? One reason is that we may tell ourselves God cannot be trusted in this matter and will overreact. Another possibility is that we may secretly doubt the boundlessness of His forgiveness, as complete exoneration seems untenable in our critical thinking. For many of us it is quite easy in the emotional turmoil of the moment to confuse his loving fatherly discipline with rejection. All these reasons skew our perception of our Father as the one who forgives and embraces the lost without limit and without exception.

Meanwhile, our Father is waiting patiently with washing soda in one hand and a pitcher of fresh water in the other hand to cleanse us of our shame and disgrace. As soon as we grow tired of playing with the dry bones in Ezekiel's valley, He will begin His work in earnest. His standing invitation to all of us, always, is "'Come now, let us settle the matter,' says the LORD, 'Though your sins are like scarlet they shall be as white as snow; though they are red as crimson, they shall be like wool'" (Isaiah 1:18). In other words, let us hand over the dirty glass of shame and disgrace to our Father and He will make us sparkle as our hearts are filled with the joy and love that comes from our Father's forgiveness.

His forgiveness, made possible through the blood of Christ, means we no longer need to fear eternal rejection. In the place of shame and disgrace is an open door to a warm hearth, a cup of fine drink, and the tender- hearted embrace of a Savior who calls us "friend." It is a deep and life fulfilling friendship forged on a wooden cross and iron-spiked hands and feet. There is neither a need to fear rejection nor a need to strive to please Him. So let go of the dry bones and your fear of rejection and come to your Father with an open heart! He is waiting to pour His love into you!

Father, I have been hiding from You long enough. I have mistakenly feared Your rejection of me. How foolish I have been. I want to come home. Here I am. Search me and make me whole. I lay down whatever You bring to my mind_____. Thank You for freeing me, forgiving me, and overwhelming me with Your love and acceptance. Amen.

Meditation: Jesus replied, "Very truly I tell you, everyone who sins is a slave to sin. Now a slave has no permanent place in the family, but a son belongs to it forever. So if the Son sets you free, you will be free indeed." (John 8:34–36)

Worship: "Holy Water" (We the Kingdom)

Tips: Our Father knows our fears and doubts that arise in the back of our minds. He wants us to have the confidence and freedom to know we are truly forgiven and sin no longer needs to rule over us and rob us of the security of His love and acceptance. Tell your Father what is frightening you. Be blunt! His voice is always life-giving, able to correct, and overflow our hearts with love and gratitude simultaneously.

*Wait for the L*ORD*; be strong and take heart and wait for the* LORD.

Psalm 27:14

RECORKING A CHAMPAGNE BOTTLE

The Dry Bones of Fearing God's Timing

Popping the cork of a Champagne bottle and letting it fly is one of life's grandest traditions. It can also be dangerous to partygoers or family heirlooms that happen to be in the path of the flying cork. The CO_2 in the bottle causes the cork to launch and is the reason behind the mushroom-shaped design of the cork. A wire cage wrapped around the cork and bottle securely holds the CO_2 inside until you release it. But what happens if someone opens the bottle a week before the proper time? For those of us who have thought about recorking the Champagne bottle, the task is impossible, since the base of the cork is significantly wider than the opening of the Champagne bottle. That's the dilemma once you open it—there is no way to close it apart from having a Champagne corking machine around, which most of us don't have. Ultimately you end up with bottle of Champagne without bubbles before the festivities start. How depressing! Its grand opening should have waited!

Recorking a Champagne bottle is not the only thing that is impossible. There are some things in life that once uncorked cannot be changed through human effort. It is an area of life that brings heartache and sadness. We may find that we have been trying to use the bones in Ezekiel's valley to pound that cork back into the bottle without any success. How many of us echo the words of Mary to our Lord, "If you had been here, my *brother [sister, daughter, son, friend, mother, father]* would not have . . ." (John 11:32, emphasis added).

The grief can be so overwhelming that it is both natural and tempting to find something to soothe the deep pain. As we are looking for healing, we may soon discover other bottles in the world, the material and human kind, that offer us a bottle with an opening the same size as the Champagne cork. Everything seems just right to comfort and satisfy our deepest hurts. The pull is strong, and the invitation is compelling, but in our hearts we hear the warning of God, *Do you want only what you want or do you want My best?* If we continue to go our own route, the pain will be even greater because those other bottles were not designed to hold the Champagne of God's healing. We must wait on God's timing for God's healing.

Waiting upon God's timing is one of the hardest lessons in life. It can create great fear and anxiety, especially when waiting involves someone or something dear to our hearts. Waiting upon God requires several difficult things from us. First, we need to recognize God's timing is always the best timing. It may not seem like it, but it will always prove true. Second, we need to surrender our images of how and when things are going to unfold. God will always do the unexpected and His unexpected is always superior to anything we could ever dream. Finally, we need Scriptures to which we can cling tightly and persevere in prayer until He uses His Word to intervene.

Remember, no matter how much we try to change the situation, our efforts will prove to be fruitless, and our sense of hopelessness will increase. God's Word teaches us that it is "'not by might nor by power, but by my Spirit,' says the LORD Almighty" (Zechariah 4:6) that the uncorkable corks of our lives are healed. Choose to walk with the Healer in peace instead of waiting in fear and dread. Waste no more moments looking for poor substitutes and determine in your heart to trust Him and His perfect timing.

Lord, these are the things that are troubling my heart_____. I ask You to heal each of them. Please provide me a promise from Your perfect Word that I may hold on to with all my heart. I know You will be faithful and fulfill that promise at Your appointed time. Bring that promise to mind whenever I become anxious and help me persevere in prayer even when my eyes do not see any movement nor change in the situation. Amen.

Meditation: Wait for the LORD; be strong and take heart and wait for the LORD. (Psalm 27:14)

Worship: "Healing Rain" (Michael W. Smith) or "Scars in Heaven" (Casting Crowns)

Tips: Waiting on God is hard work. Go easy on yourself and share your heart with a close friend, spouse, or counselor. Meditate on Scripture and write down your thoughts. Find things that are constructive while you wait, such as exercise, dinner with friends, support groups, and anything or anyone that God places on your heart. God's unexpected happens in the midst of these things.

Teach us to number our days, that we may gain a heart of wisdom.

Psalm 90:12

DAY 30

AN EMPTY CHAMPAGNE BOTTLE

The Dry Bones of Fearing a Life Lived in Vain

New Year's Day, across the globe, millions of people are waking up to a house full of dirty dishes and partially filled glasses, leftover food, streamers and horns as well as empty bottles of soda, wine, distilled liquor, and, of course, Champagne. Well, after some breakfast, it is time to clean up! Dishes, glasses, and silverware into the dishwasher! Leftover food into the waste can! Cans and bottles into the recycle bin! Now you are done and have time to enjoy the rest of the day! Hold on! You probably haven't given any thought to this, but as you were putting that Champagne bottle into the recycle bin did you consider that this bottle once held special meaning to you in the wee hours of that very morning? It was less than twelve hours removed from chilling in your refrigerator waiting with anticipation for the clock to strike midnight! What once held such joy and promise as you celebrated the end of one year and ushered in the New Year with its promises of hope and new beginnings is now in your hand, empty! About to be cast away into the recycle bin! Worthless in your eyes! It is kind of sad, isn't it?

When you consider the journey that each Champagne bottle has taken to get into our hands on New Year's Eve, we may never want to open one. Consider that some vines have been planted one to two generations ago and have endured decades of winters and annual pruning cycles. Or consider the years of toil being poured into caring for each vineyard. Then there is the year(s) that the grapes used to make our bottle of Champagne were harvested, pressed, fermented, bottled, and aged according to meticulous quality standards of each Champagne house. All these things happened before that bottle was allowed to be packed upon a truck and ultimately find its way to our local wine shops. Now, on the morning of the New Year that bottle sits empty in a recycle bin waiting for its last journey. I bet you will never look at a Champagne bottle the same way again!

In many ways the journey of a Champagne bottle can be an allegory of our own journey in life. Though our journey may last several generations, in the end we are only here but for a moment and then we are gone. Death overtakes all of us and the mistake we can make is pursuing things in this world that have no eternal value. We would be wise to heed the experience of King Solomon who investigated this issue for us "to see what was worthwhile for people to do under the heavens during the few days of their lives" (Ecclesiastes 2:3). He undertook massive projects, acquired enormous wealth, and received fame and honor. In his final assessment he concluded:

> I denied myself nothing my eyes desired; I refused
> my heart no pleasure. My heart took delight in all

> my labor and this was the reward for all my toil.
> Yet when I surveyed all that my hands had done
> and what I had toiled to achieve, everything was
> meaningless, a chasing after the wind; nothing was
> gained under the sun. (Ecclesiastes 2:10–11)

Stunning! In an attempt to find meaning in the things this world had to offer, he found them to be without worth. One of the most tragic paths we can follow is the long, dusty, and arduous trail Solomon took that ends directly in front of the entrance to Ezekiel's valley of dry bones. Each thing the world offers us is one step closer to Solomon's trail of regret. Each day we continue to journey on this trail will only exasperate our fear that we are ultimately living this life in vain. The longer we hike this trail the harder it will be to exit. It is at this point we need to hear our Savior's voice, "I came that they may have life and have it abundantly" (John 10:10 ESV). This is the alternative trail that leads to a life of substance and eternal worth.

There are three things required that will give our lives the worth we are seeking. First, we must recognize the meaning of the empty tomb of Christ. It is the validation of God's love for each of us. Apart from the empty tomb, the cross is void of its power to atone for our sins and mend our relationship with God. It is God's love that declares we are not worthless and it is God's love that pulls us to Him to confess, repent, and believe the good news of Christ.

Second, we must recognize the truth of Solomon's final words—having found the right place to look for meaning after searching in all the wrong places: "Fear God and keep his commandments, for this is the duty of all mankind" (Ecclesiastes 12:13). Jesus put it very succinctly, "If you love me, keep my commands" (John 14:15). Obedience to God and love of God are inseparable. It is the best choice, though the hardest choice, for it ensures a life ripe with eternal fruitfulness, worth, and value (John 15:1–17).

Third, delight ourselves in God. The psalmist wrote, "Take delight in the LORD and he will give you the desires of your heart" (Psalm 37:4). Enjoy the life He gives to you! Treat everything as a temporary gift from your Father's hand. Desire His presence wherever you go and whatever you do and joy will overwhelm your heart! Remember, this world is not your home! It is with our Father and our Lord and Savior, Jesus.

A life lived in the center of the love of Christ is a life that can never be lived in vain.

Father, my soul finds its worth in You alone! Where I have allowed the pursuits of this world to enchant my heart, please bring them to the open. Forgive me and show me the way I should go! I want my life to be filled with eternal significance and each day You give me to overflow with Your eternal love. Amen.

Meditation: Teach us to number our days, that we may gain a heart of wisdom. (Psalm 90:12)

Also reflect on the entire book of Ecclesiastes.

Worship: "He Knows My Name" (Francesca Battistelli)

Tips: Take a walk through a graveyard and consider its meaning. Look at the tombstones and consider the lives these people may have lived. We will join them; they will not join us. Allow God to impress upon your heart how to live going forward knowing your days are few so that your remaining days may be the most meaningful days in the sight of your Father.

"Whoever serves me must follow me; and where I am, my servant also will be. My Father will honor the one who serves me."

John 12:26

DAY 31

A TRANSPLANTED VINE

A Renewed Life Requires Being a Servant of Jesus

One of the vineyard operations that takes place every year in Champagne is the replacing of dead or unproductive vines with new vines. Typically, the new vines are grown in a dedicated place on the property or on a nearby farm that supplies the industry. When they are old enough, they will be dug up, roots clipped, and moved to the new location where the old vine has been uprooted. The young vine is then buried and generously watered to saturate its roots with sufficient water. Special care must be given to these new plantings until the root system is fully established and the main stock of the plant is able to grow. It is a very routine and standard procedure.

However, from the plant's perspective, this process is a dramatic experience. It awakens in the early morning finding the once-friendly gardener who sang beautiful songs to the plant, now is tearing up its comfortable soil bed. Then its roots get clipped (ouch!) by this so-called friend. Recklessly tossed into an unfamiliar hole in an unfamiliar land, the vineyard manager then buries the young vine and nearly drowns it in water. The vine's nice cozy life in the nursery is now over. But as the vine recovers from the shock and while the memories of the old place still linger, it may look around at its new home, among the mighty and prestigious vines of Champagne and realize its new home is indeed very good. It will conclude in its mind that the vineyard manager is a pretty good friend after all, much wiser than itself, for the kindly gardener who still sings the beautiful melodies of its youth had deemed the plant worthy to be grown in a place where the grapes are the finest, the sparkling wine is the grandest, and the name is without equal. The place of Champagne!

A servant of Christ! It does not sound like an important title from the world's perspective. And even within church circles, where we have pastors, bishops, cardinals, elders, evangelists, deacons, seminary professors, and other such titles, the idea of "a servant of Jesus" does not communicate or immediately fit our mold of someone with great importance, leadership ability, or authority. However, it is the only title of importance to our Lord. We are either servants of Jesus or we are not!

While speaking to His disciples concerning the imminence of His death on the cross as well as the requirements to be His disciple, Jesus said,

> "Very truly I tell you, unless a kernel of wheat falls to the ground and dies, it remains only a single seed. But if it dies, it produces many seeds. Anyone who loves their life will lose it, while anyone who hates their life in this world will keep it for eternal

life. Whoever serves me must follow me; and
where I am, my servant also will be. My Father will
honor the one who serves me." (John 12:24–26)

His words to us should cause each of us to stop. Any notion
that we are more than just mere servants of Christ is instantaneously dispelled with eight simple words from our Lord:
"where I am, my servant also will be." And to be where He
is requires one thing from us—which is the hardest thing for
us to do—surrendering our wills for our Father's will!

Our Lord set before all of us the standard for what it
means to surrender our wills to the will of our Father, when
in the garden of Gethsemane Jesus prayed, "Father, if you
are willing, take this cup from me; yet not my will, but yours
be done" (Luke 22:42). We all have areas in our lives we
know are not fully surrendered to our Father. Yet this path
of "not my will, but yours" is exactly where we need to be if
we want to be servants of Jesus.

The unsurrendered area of our lives may involve a relationship, an activity, our work, or even our wealth. It may
involve a sin in our lives that keeps tripping us up. Maybe it
is how we use our time each day and we realize we have not
given sufficient energy toward prayer, reading Scripture, or
serving others. Whatever area(s) that requires surrendering
to the Lord, let Him bring it to mind. But when He does,
we will face one of the greatest battles of our lives as every
inch of us wants to hold onto that thing and not give it over
to our Lord. This is the point where fear, doubts, trust issues
with God, or our desire to maintain the "cozy life of the
nursery" will emerge, fighting against the will of our Father.

However, during this fight to fully surrender, let us consider to whom we are surrendering our lives. God is not a
tyrant who wants to harm us and desires our destruction, like
Satan. Just the opposite, God is the One who spoke

everything into existence, made it beautiful and good, and deliberately made us the pinnacle of His creative energy and attention. We are surrendering to our heavenly Father. We are not an afterthought. God *wanted* us. He wanted a family filled with many children—children that are of great joy and delight, all made in the image of His Son.

Is there anyone in this world who loves you more than your heavenly Father? There is none! Until we are fully convinced of this truth and respond by surrendering our will to His, we will never experience His lasting peace and the assurance we are truly in His perfect will.

So let us waste no more precious time and bow our hearts and surrender to His good will. Allow our Lord the good pleasure to uproot us from the limited confines of the "cozy nursery" and plant us among the prestigious vines of His grand and glorious vineyard, where all who are planted bear the same name, Servant of Jesus.

Father, reveal to me any area of my life that is not fully surrendered to Your good will. Give me the courage to release the following area of my life into Your loving hands: _____. I know by surrendering that area to You I will finally have peace in that area of my life. I now surrender . . . If there is anything else that now needs to take place, including actions I need to take to make my surrender complete, reveal that to me. Now, my Father, may my only desire in life be that of a good and faithful servant of Jesus. Amen!

Meditation: "Very truly I tell you, unless a kernel of wheat falls to the ground and dies, it remains only a single seed. But if it dies, it produces many seeds. Anyone who loves their life will lose it, while anyone who hates their life in this world will keep it for eternal life. Whoever serves me must follow me; and where I am, my servant also will be. My Father will honor the one who serves me." (John 12:24–26).

Worship Song: "At the Cross" (Chris Tomlin)

Tips: Surrender takes time! It is not instantaneous! Jesus took at least an hour to surrender His will to His Father prior to being arrested, beaten, and crucified (Matthew 26:40). Some decisions are so life-changing that you need to take the time to wrestle with God about them to ensure you heard correctly. However, once you understand what He has asked of you, then it is by faith you surrender.

The greatest adventures of your life all start the moment you choose to surrender!

Do everything without grumbling or arguing, so that you may become blameless and pure, "children of God without fault in a crooked and depraved generation." Then you will shine among them like stars in the sky as you hold firmly to the word of life.

Philippians 2:14–16a

EPILOGUE

Remuage! This is a French word meaning riddling, which is a technique for gathering all the sediment at the neck of the bottle prior to disgorging. It is this technique that produces the perfectly clear glass of Champagne without any imperfection that we all expect and enjoy. Think of these 31 daily readings as a form of remuage on your life where you allow God to filter out everything in your life that is dead and lifeless.

There will be areas where the sediment appears to be caked onto the bottle and pose a great difficulty to disgorge. However, holding onto even a little sediment—whether harboring it in our minds, hearts, or actions—will deprive us of the clarity, peace, and contentment we long for and desire. So, if you have grown tired of holding onto that sediment, take courage! Refocus your attention on Jesus. Let God remove the sediment so you can sparkle with the fullness of Christ shining brightly into your heart and through your life to your joy and to your Father's glory.

ENDNOTES

1. Theologically referred to as the doctrine of the Trinity, Scripture teaches there is one God, who exists eternally in three distinct "persons"—Father, Son, and Holy Spirit—who are completely equal and who are each fully God.
2. Academy Award for Best Picture in 1966.
3. *Terroir* is a French term that captures the unique set of variables that influences the characteristics—taste, aroma, acidity, etc.—of each Champagne. Those variables include the weather, climate, soil, Champagne-making techniques, and grape variety. In essence, it's the Champagne's home—a distinct place with a distinct Champagne-making tradition—that produces a distinct Champagne.
4. Price in the year 2019.

ABOUT THE AUTHOR

 ryan A. Anderson spends his time between Oregon and the East Coast where he focuses his time on the spiritual revival of the banking and securities industry. He holds degrees from the University of Pennsylvania, Columbia University, Gordon Conwell Theological Seminary, and an Intermediate Certificate with Distinction from the WSET (2010, International Wine Center, New York City). Bryan has over 30 years experience in the banking and securities industry and has worked for some of the largest banking and securities firms in the world.

RESOURCES

1. Coombe, Brian and Peter Dry, ed. *Viticulture: Volume 2 Practices.* Ashford, South Australia: Winetitles Pry LTD, 2008.

2. Mazzeo, Tilar J. *The Widow Clicquot: The Story of a Champagne Empire and the Woman Who Ruled It.* New York: Harper Perennial, 2008.

3. McCarthy, Ed. *Champagne For Dummies.* Foster City, CA: IDG Books Worldwide, 1999.

4. Stevenson, Tom and Essi Avellan MW. *Christie's World Encyclopedia of Champagne & Sparkling Wine.* New York: Sterling Epicure, 2014.

5. *See* Veuveclicquot.com *for more on the history of this Champagne house.*

6. For more on Madame Clicquot's fascinating story, see Natasha Geiling, "The Widow Who Created the Champagne Industry," Smithsonian Magazine, November 2013, https://www.smithsonianmag.com/arts-culture/the-widow-who-created-the-champagne-industry-180947570/.

7. https://www.champagne.fr/en

8. https://www.decanter.com

9. https://maisons-champagne.com/en